HUMAN NATURE UNDER GOD

HUMAN NATURE UNDER GOD

OR *Adventure of Personality*

BY OREN HULING BAKER, Ph.D.

*Dean and Albert W. Beaven Professor
of Pastoral Theology at the
Colgate Rochester Divinity School
Rochester, New York*

ASSOCIATION PRESS · NEW YORK

TO MY WIFE, MARGARET,
AND MY DAUGHTERS,
ELIZABETH ANN AND MARY ELLEN

ACKNOWLEDGMENTS

IN ADDITION TO ACKNOWLEDGMENTS appropriately made in the documentation of the text of this book, I wish to recognize the special courtesy of the Division of Christian Education of the National Council of Churches of Christ for permission to quote from the Revised Standard Version of the Old and New Testaments. I owe similar debt to The Macmillan Company, The Ronald Press Company, Charles Scribner's Sons, W. W. Norton & Company, Inc., Curtis Brown, Ltd., all of New York; to the University of Chicago Press of Chicago, Illinois, and to The Pastoral Psychology Press of Great Neck, New York. I am grateful to these publishers for allowing quotations from their copyrighted works named in the footnotes and listed in the Bibliography.

To others who have been closer to me in this venture and shared the toil, I owe much more than can be described. Dr. Ernest W. Parsons, Professor Emeritus of New Testament Interpretation at Colgate Rochester Divinity School, Dr. J. Alvin Sanders, currently Assistant Professor of Old Testament Interpretation in the same institution, Dr. John

R. Slater, who had a long and distinguished career as Professor of English Literature at the University of Rochester, and Professor Charles L. Wallis of Keuka College read the entire manuscript and offered invaluable criticisms. Dr. Benjamin Pollack, psychiatrist and Assistant Director of the Rochester State Hospital, examined Chapters 6 and 7 for technical accuracy. The patience and care of Miss Marcia Woodworth in making numerous revisions and putting the work in its final form were an unfailing help.

I wish to mention also the kindness of Dean James Cannon III of the Duke University Divinity School in extending to me the hospitality of that institution during my residence there in the spring of 1955 when this work was begun. My gratitude goes also to Mr. John P. Waggoner, Librarian of Duke University, for his service in putting at my disposal the facilities under his direction.

OREN H. BAKER
Rochester, New York

CONTENTS

INTRODUCTION

> *Religion is the art and the theory of the internal life of man, so far as it depends on the man himself and on what is permanent in the nature of things.*[1]

RELIGION IS MAN'S QUEST FOR ASSURANCE that he can live by faith and love while doubt and fear lay siege to his heart. It is his attempt to resolve inward dilemma by organizing his relations with the world in a way that will serve his need for security and fulfillment. It is the search for what is enduring in time and eternity.

No fact, however, is more conspicuous in the history of religion than human discontent with what is offered at any time as a final formulation of faith. Sometimes this reaction is directed toward institutional forms and practices; sometimes it involves a questioning of beliefs and a distrust of the effectiveness of religion in producing personal and cultural change. Not infrequently it centers in the more

---

[1] Alfred North Whitehead, *Religion in the Making*, p. 16. New York: The Macmillan Company, 1926. Used by permission of the publisher.

general issue of the total relevance of religion to the problems of the common life. Emphasis varies with occasion, and combinations of all these are common. Examples of this tendency may be found in any period of the Christian era; but, for our purposes, we need go no further for illustration than our own recent history in America.

At the beginning of the century, two main issues, already familiar in Europe, were demanding a reorientation of religious thought. One arose from the challenge of modern science, the other from the "social crisis" precipitated by the effects of new ways in industrial production that had been gaining ground since the Civil War. In the first, the problem was seen to be mainly intellectual; in the second, it lay in practical affairs and called for the application of ethical principles, institutional reforms, and governmental regulation. Both were engaging serious attention in the colleges, universities, and professional schools where leadership for the common life was in training. Religious thinkers sought to meet the questions posed by science through a reconstruction of the religious view of the world in such a way as to assimilate the newer views emerging from laboratories and lecture rooms. This was essentially a repetition of what had happened in earlier periods as a result of the discoveries of Galileo, Copernicus, Newton, and others. In this more recent instance, however, the issue struck closer to man than the former which had been concerned with the nature of the physical world. Startling though it was to discover the errors in the Ptolemaic system upon which the medieval conception of the universe had been formed, it soon became apparent that the new knowledge did not drastically affect man's view of himself. After all, his prestige was manifest in the work of his hands and his increasing dominion over the earth. Soon the scientists themselves were helping this cause. They reported that the precision of their instruments and their most profound speculations could not produce evidence of the existence of any creatures comparable to human beings in all stellar space. The dictum, "We are all there is of us," was enough to keep back straight, chest out, and chin up.

But deflation was on the way. The theory of evolution plowed deeper ground. It demanded a revolutionary change in man's conception of his origin and nature. The fact of the earth's position as one of the minor planets could be endured, but this new thing—in idea actually very old—stirred up by Charles Darwin in 1859 was a body blow, some said "insult," to the human ego.

Nevertheless, theologians, aided by half a century of research which had put the Bible in historical perspective, went to work on the problem and by the end of the century had made great progress in relating the new scientific doctrine to the religious outlook. Notable among these, to mention only one, was William Newton Clarke's *Outline of Christian Theology,* published in 1899, in which the intellectual synthesis was practically completed.[2] At that time, however, few folk in the churches were even aware of the problem; and the emotional adjustment, always in

---

[2] *The Outline of Christian Theology,* pp. 222-226. New York: Charles Scribner's Sons, 1899.

arrears, waited for a much longer period, which was to be marked by outbursts of extreme protest.

The social crisis was felt most acutely in the cities where economic deprivation took heavy toll in sweatshops and child labor. It was here that the Judeo-Christian conscience was stirred into action. Social work had its beginnings in these years, while pastors in their daily round found disease and poverty in virulent forms and began to preach and write about the shame of these evils in a land richly endowed with physical and human resources adequate to meet all normal needs. The interest of the clergy in the labor movement stemmed directly from what they saw in their parishes. The thinking of such men as Walter Rauschenbusch, Washington Gladden, Graham Taylor, Francis J. McConnell, and Stephen S. Wise expressed the religious reaction to these conditions.

But the crisis was not limited to the United States. It had its counterpart in Europe, and notably in Japan where industrialization was making phenomenal strides. Eventually the distress within nations, accompanied by political measures of various kinds and the continued acceleration of social change by advancing inventive genius, led to two world wars entailing colossal destruction and to an economic depression of world-wide proportions. The response of the religious mind was immediate and drastic. What Darwin had done to man by the doctrine of evolution was a mere abstract pin-prick compared with what Hitler did to disclose the volcanic nature of human dynamics. By the torture of the helpless, by the massacre of whole communities, and by the vaporization of populous cities man found himself in a state of regression that shook his self-esteem and gave rise to new views about "nonbeing" and "nothingness." The world, especially Europe, was ready for the forthcoming theology of despair. The dogma that "man is a sinner" was announced with new emphasis as though it had never been heard of before, the old flirtation with total depravity was resumed and, with the hydrogen bomb in the offing, the topic of the day became *eschata*, or "last things." Theology was again changing with the cultural seasons. "Queen of the sciences" she still claimed to be, but her record continued to show a succession of abdications and coronations; "of the sciences"—that stood in question.

The mood induced by change inaugurates the quest for foundations that remain unshaken, for that which "is permanent in the nature of things." [3] The religious mind looks for this in two main directions. It turns first to the institution that has nurtured it, hoping to find a temple of refuge where it can recover strength to ease the pain of spiritual dislocation and disillusionment. For many, this is sufficient. But to the more sensitive, the shock of events turns a critical eye upon the claims and forms handed down from the past. Mere rewording is not enough. The search must go deeper, even to the foundations of the institution itself. Life must be rethought within an ampler and more rigorous framework that will uncover the sources of failure and offer better reason for hope. This, for most devout

---

[3] Whitehead, Alfred N., *op. cit.*

people of the Occident, leads to the Bible. Here, however, the answers are not found in terms directly related to the questions which press upon the modern mind. The literature is vast, and the categories of thought belong to a time far removed from the thinking in which the day's work is done. There is advantage in the fact that the Bible has entered into the warp and woof of our ideological fabric and has gathered around it strong sentiments which support confidence in it. But these may have the effect also of closing the doors of understanding by a too easy reading of what is written there and by the necessity of every man hearing in his own language if he is to hear at all. The problem of making the message of the Bible available, in a more important sense than numerical distribution, is therefore a continuing one. To this objective many of our best minds are directing their efforts. A survey of the field reveals at least three major approaches to the problem.

Foremost stands the work of the biblical scholars who in the past one hundred years have attained a result of monumental proportions and put the religious world under a debt which will remain unpaid as long as interest in knowing the truth continues. High intelligence, patience, and skill have been applied so thoroughly that scarcely a jot or tittle of the record has escaped scrutiny. This service has not been limited to the study of the documents which lie in and behind the books of the canon and the extra-canonical literature. The pick and shovel of the archeologist have filled many gaps in the history, provided corroboration for events vaguely known, and added insights needed for better understanding and interpretation. Creative imagination, with a restraint that amounts to reverence in dealing with discrepancies, has made conjecture more than guess. The mandate to search the Scriptures has not only been remembered but extended to include any discovery that adds to revelation. The digging in the sterile sands of the deserts, the rummaging in old cellars and caves, the piecing together of fragments of potsherds and papyri have been motivated by the desire better to understand human nature. By discerning how it behaved in the past, how it shaped the course of culture, new light is sought on the problem of man's perception and control of himself.

This motive is not peculiar to modern research, for it has been characteristic of men in every age when they have inquired about the meaning of their existence. Indeed, it was the need of the Jewish people and the early Christians to know about their past in order to meet the demands of their current hour that led to the collection of the books contained in the Bible. Both of the Testaments were formed to serve the interests of religious communities that already existed. There is a sense, then, in which modern scholarship, in its relation to present-day religion, has its counterpart in ancient times. In a word, its contribution to making the Bible available consists mainly in telling us what it *was* in the first place. This is indispensable foundation.

The second approach to the problem undertakes to answer the question concerning what the Bible *is*. This is the task to which the theologian sets himself and which has special importance for Protestants because of their historic reliance on the Bible for authority in matters of faith. The theologian undertakes to relate the findings of biblical scholars to the thought of his own time as that thought expresses itself in philosophy, literature, and science. It is a formal, reasoned, systematic result that he seeks. His work may be weighted on one side or the other, but in so far as he makes appeal to the Bible it is his aim to translate its meanings into terms which "justify the ways of God" to modern men. He stands between the mind of the ancient world and the modern mind as mediator. For this reason he must devise concepts through which the meanings of both may flow.

An example of this is found in the idea of the "Word of God." This expression is susceptible to several interpretations. It may mean what the scholars say it meant in its original setting. It may mean the literal word of Scripture. More often, in our time, it does not refer exclusively to either of these, but to a Word which unites all particular and relevant passages. The process is similar to looking at the racial diversity of mankind and then speaking of it as the Life of Man. We call such an expression "generic" in that it lifts out the common elements and neglects the differences. In a similar manner, the theologian seems to say that there is a generic Word which permeates the particular words. In this way, he frees himself from the limitations of the ancient world view and establishes connections between it and the thinking of modern men by a kind of invisible line of communication. We call this the generalizing tendency of the mind. In the theologian's perspective, however, this is seen as man's mode of approach to meanings which have their source outside of his own thought and ultimately assume the character of personal encounter with God.

The third approach to the Bible stems from the incentive to *use* it. This is related to both the preceding interests as they are to it. The practical interest, traditionally designated pastoral theology, centers, however, on the problem in the last and most acute phase presented by the actual functioning of the Bible in the experience of living men. It comes to sharpest focus and test in the work of the Christian pastor and teacher as they meet people in the face-to-face relations of pulpit, classroom, and parish. This is where the real crisis comes. The scholar and the systematic theologian are concerned mainly with the gathering and classification of data, the drawing of inferences, evaluation of ideas, and the use of concepts in formulating a body of knowledge having broad relevance to human needs. The datum for the practical theologian is the person *in situ*. It is his chief concern to relate more directly the formal thinking about religion to the dynamic character of the human beings whom he daily serves. The sciences of man—anthropology, sociology, and especially psychology—bear the same relation to his work that philosophy bears to his colleague who is seeking a synthesis of valid beliefs.

When, however, the practical theologian with this orientation comes to the Bible, he discovers that from beginning to end there is hardly a single formal treatise on any subject. Instead, it teems with concrete situations in which men, through successive generations, engage in inward battle marked by an intensity and persistence rarely found elsewhere in the annals of mankind. It is the story of an undaunted race whose struggles alternate between "blood, sweat, and tears" and songs of hope that pierce the shadows until the dawn comes. The Bible is God's parish where every conceivable evil stalks and where suffering to overcome it wades in the mud of the Euphrates and finally mounts a cross. The most formal thing about the Book is its canonization. Otherwise, it is life in all the diversity, discreteness, variability, and contradiction that are the marks of men everywhere. In it we see human nature as in a mirror.

It is in the field of this third concern that the present work is undertaken. Briefly stated, our thesis is that religion is integral with the adventure of personality. It is our view that religion arises in man because of the unique fact of his self-consciousness, his capacity to perceive the meanings of his own existence and undertake the direction of his life through a free collaboration with God in loyalty to "one increasing purpose" which "through the ages runs." The central focus of our interest is in the inner life as the seat of decision where divergent claims are reconciled and the course of redemptive fulfillment chosen. The treatment of this theme falls into two parts. Part I traces the development of religion in the soul of Israel from Abraham to Paul. The term "soul" is used in its essential Hebrew sense. It refers to the life as a whole, the total animate creature, and conforms essentially to our conception of mind-body organism. Part II deals with human nature from the standpoint of modern knowledge, especially psychology. Here the subject is Man the Person. The unifying principle in the entire work is the concept of self-consciousness as it appears in successive contexts presented by our data.

In the unfolding of the thought of this book, it is important to understand why biblical material occupies almost half the space. Some of the reasons for this have already been intimated. Most significant of all is the fact that the Holy Scriptures become an indispensable text when an examination of the inner life is undertaken from a religious point of view. Rooted in history and expressing the engagement of a particular people with objective conditions of their environing world, the Bible long ago passed beyond that history into universal literature. In this character, it has the value of an epic of the soul whose range encompasses moods of the spirit which are common to men everywhere. It is, therefore, inescapable as a source for discerning the nature of religion and appraising its continuing function in the renewal and redirection of life which every generation needs. It is not enough, however, just to say this. The truth must be discovered in the literal concreteness of events through which the Bible speaks. For this reason we assign a large place to biblical data. The record, as we use it, is of necessity compressed and drawn to the purpose in hand but, even so, the full story must be told in order to make clear the points at issue and to preserve the integrity of its original intention.

As a part of this task, it should be emphasized also that although concepts derived from psychology are employed in our treatment of the subject matter, deliberate effort is made to avoid using the Bible to substantiate psychological theories. Psychology, at best, is a tool to guide understanding, not master or determining canon in the normative sense. In brief, the aims of our undertaking seem better advanced by an inductive method which allows the Bible, as primary text, to present first the evidence concerning the nature of the inner life, as we do in Part I, with only that degree of illumination which is necessary along the way to keep the subject in focus. Then, more directly, we turn in Part II to the human story as it is set forth in the modern sciences of man. The bond between these two divisions of our work is supplied by concepts which are relevant to both and lead to the outcomes of the closing chapters.

Central in our understanding of the inner life, as we see it in the Bible and in psychology, is the distinction drawn between the self and the person. In our view, these terms describe different aspects of the soul. The first acknowledges the social origin of personality; the second designates the individual's unique reactions to social experience in the search for meaning and destiny. The person is grounded in the self and draws upon its resources, as mind relies upon brain and body, but these are related to purposes beyond self. The self finds support in the society which nurtures it; the person seeks companionship beyond society in God. Corollary to this is the sense of social obligation, on the one hand, and the need to express one's responsibility for the total adventure of man, on the other. The person thus unites concern for neighbor with devotion to God.

Part I should be read in this light to discern that the abiding significance of the Bible is found in its disclosure of the struggle of man the self, to become man the person. A good illustration of what this means appears in the story of King Saul. Here Israel, as a "self" among other nations, seeks security and realization of ambition by political means, while Israel, as a "person," judges the acts of self by affirming the claims of Yahweh and a higher destiny. The example suggests also that mental illness is the result of defects in the constitution of the self which threaten the growth, freedom, and maturity of the person. The "evil spirit" in Saul is a symbol of this. In like manner, the judgments and faith of the prophets express the insistent demand of man's nature to fulfill itself in personhood. Insights related to this theme emerge on almost every page of our study and move with cumulative effect toward culmination in Jesus. The fuller and more contemporary implications are rounded out, as we said, in Part II.

A special word about time may be useful to the reader as he follows the thought of the writer in these pages. In the chapters dealing with the biblical material, the historical present tense is used almost entirely. There are two reasons for this. In the first place, the Bible is a normal part of all our thinking about religion. It speaks directly to us and, in so far as it is revelation in a vital sense, it reflects our own search for the true and the good. This gives it relevance to our personal adventure. It is in us and we are in it. In the second place, the history of the soul is an inference from events just as other history is. For us, however, the focus is on the inner event rather than the outer.

Time, in our thinking, is more than intervals set off from one another like figures on a dial. It is more than a calendar of dates. It is movement more than measure, movement in the substance of occasions uniting quality with quantity. It is more *kairos,* in the sense of "appropriate season," than *chronos*. It is like morning awakening with the stir of the ox coming to his crib, the singing of a bird, the bleating of a lamb, the crying of a child; like evening with weariness folding into sleep, fading light on the hill, darkness over the valley, the call of the owl, the shining of the stars. Time is the day with everything in it; the night and all it portends. It is the act where man meets nature, the members of his household, and his neighbor. It is the feeling of nearness in distant memory, gone but clinging to and a part of the present. It is alternation between fact and fancy, between belief and doubt, hope and despair. Time is inward spacing, the change of stress in the substance of the soul. It is crisis marking a moment of creation that is shadowed by destruction and waiting for the movement of the Spirit of the Eternal over impending chaos. Time is our life recapitulating the past in our present moment and reaching toward the future. It is the expanding boundaries of our adventure.

PART I   *The Soul of Israel*

1. THE EARLY YEARS

1. *Adventure Begins—Individuality*

IN THE CRADLE OF THE ANCIENT EAST, rocked by winds blown from the desert over the "fertile crescent," the soul of Israel was born. "Get thee out" are the words which mark a beginning that follows an ending inscribed with brief finality on a tomb in Haran—"Terah died." Behind the old camp lies the distant past, mystery receding with the sands of time and leaving mirages of memory to give substance to forgotten origins. Westward destiny calls to a land unknown and a future bounded by uncertainty. But the promise of widening horizons, confirmed by inward conviction, overcomes hesitation and evokes response to the mandate of history, "Walk before me, and be thou perfect." The mode of travel is important. Walking is realism. It expresses the true pace of the inner life, no matter what other means may be used to close the gaps in traversing physical distance.

On occasion, imagination may swiftly surmount all barriers and anticipate what is yet unachieved in actual event;

but soon the touch with reality is regained, and the soul, earthbound, continues on foot. This is what it means to be in history. There is no sudden flight from start to finish, no speeding up of inward growth, no precipitate result in the making of a man. Every experience, every contact with the external world, must be tested step by step joining past with present, reaching out toward the future, and weaving all together in a pattern which is uniquely shaped, never copied. Alternatives are available, but it is a law of the soul that it must be true to itself. So "Abram journeyed, going on."

He does not, however, go alone or empty-handed. There are resources in the inheritance of the father's house, kinsmen, wives and slaves, flocks and herds. These give initial security and support in the daily task and comfort when the going is tough. The closeness and warmth of loved ones sustain inward strength. But all these blessings impose responsibilities which at times weigh heavily upon the heart. When one is on his own, free to choose among the options of an open course, events must be judged warily and decision made in the light of consequences. The care of the household presents a primary claim upon time and wisdom. What is given as capital at the start is not enough. New means of subsistence must be found, and a margin of safety maintained in the face of unforeseen danger to persons and property. If human increase and fertility of the flocks confirm the dignity of manhood and add to one's wealth, there are corresponding demands upon competence.

Besides, a nomadic life requires that one be ready to strike out periodically for lands offering a new hold on opportunity. There is hazard in this, for the direction and the outcome of the journey are often obscure even when vision is clearest. The way to know is to go. Trial and error, with resolve to meet situations as they arise, have done duty through long ages and will suffice when no better rule is available. So Abram wanders at random with a hint here and there of what is ahead. First it is Shechem, then Bethel, then the Negeb or the South. Shifts are made as the ground is tested, and altars are set up at each place as signs of possession and consecration and points to which he may return if he loses his way. Altars are symbols of an overruling purpose which infuses the meanings of the far view into the passing hour and justifies the perils encountered along an uncertain way. They are places of renewal where courage returns after failure, where vision clears in the dawn after darkness, and power not one's own undergirds the will.

Nevertheless, there is no permanent respite for the soul. Recurring doubts and fears are inevitable. Abram discovers early in his journey that access to nature's bounty is attended not only by the difficulties of travel but also by the more baffling problem of human relations. The land promised to him as the place of release from the life of a wanderer is occupied by others with whom he must compete as intruder. "The Canaanite was in the land." As long as supplies are ample for all, no serious incident occurs, but when the pinch of famine comes it is the newcomer who takes the trail to Egypt. This is escape but it brings with it prospect of new peril.

Sarah, Abram's attractive wife so intimately bound up with his future fortunes, will become an object of envy among the Egyptians and his own life may be endangered. To avert this event, he plans his strategy in advance. He will say that she is his sister. The plan is carried out and when she is actually taken by Pharaoh, it proves successful for a time. When, however, the truth becomes known, he is rebuked for his ruse and dismissed from the country. In the variant on this story, recorded from another source in connection with a similar act of Abimelech, Abram adds some details to his explanation that do not appear in his words to Pharaoh. But in both instances, he rests his case on the need for self-preservation and his lack of adequate defenses in territories where the "fear of God" does not exist. By such experiences, the soul learns that fear often distorts perception and gives rise to views about other people who, in their own way, act upon standards not altogether unlike its own.

When, however, a mistake is made, one must accept it responsibly and start again at the point of error; so Abram returns to the Negeb where, in the presence of the old altar, he regains perspective and resumes his journey. By this, anxiety is allayed but not ended. There are times, especially at night, when the "horror of a great darkness" comes over the soul. Absorption in the duties of the day banishes old fears, but when one lies down to sleep they come again compounded by the memory of recent failure. Most active of all is the problem of self-perpetuation and the realization of the promise in a son. Through the open door of the tent, the eye rising above surrounding shadows beholds a sea of stars to match the inward echo, "So shall thy descendants be." The vision dims before reality. Sarah's age and apparent sterility make the thought of a child a desperate hope bordering on the ludicrous. Hagar, her handmaid, seems to be the only key to the future. At least it is wise to take this course until, perchance, Providence brings a better answer.

More immediately pressing is the problem of Lot and his household with the complications of internal rivalries and the living of too many in one place. The solution is found in the separation of the clans. This reduces the family tensions and placates the neighbors who are restive under the pressure from resourceful foreigners. When a practical decision of this sort is made, one experiences a relief that enables him to get his bearings again. A new survey of the possibilities can be taken. Abram looks to the north, the east, the south and the west. More comfortable now in himself, he can respond again to the inward call, "Arise, walk." Out of a variety of such attempts to become adjusted to environment, the soul makes progress in the art of getting along in the world.[1] At least three ways are open for developing a policy to govern human relations. One may by force clear the ground of opposition. Competitors may be expelled from the scene. A second measure may be found in using other people, subduing them, and exercising command over them as a master dealing with servants. Both of these measures require the aggressive use of power. Still an-

---

[1] Genesis 12, 13, 15-24.

other way is kindness. One may acknowledge the rights of others and win respect from them. Abram adopts the third method. Essentially a man of peace, he settles the issue with Lot by giving him first choice of the land.[2] When Sarah is no longer able to tolerate Hagar and forces her to leave, he tries to make provision for her. In this situation he has, of course, a vested interest in the child she is to bear. He avoids unnecessary interference with the Canaanites. In time, his early distrust of them abates and he can even think of adapting some of their customs to his own purposes.

When it is discovered that consideration for others actually works, because it enables one to get what he needs by allowing others to live in their own way, kindness can be generalized into a principle for future guidance. Of great importance in this process is the discovery that neighbors, though alien in many ways, are capable of reciprocating one's own acts. When this insight into the motives and intentions of other people is attained, it is possible to enter into friendly agreements which give stability to social relations. If kindness has a background of strength, restrained but real, the prospect of peaceful intercourse is even more promising. In the incident involving the taking of Sarah by Abimelech, an embarrassing beginning is brought to an end by a compact of mutual guarantees that neither of the two houses would "deal falsely" with the other. The pledge is immediately tested by Abram's complaint concerning a well which Abimelech's servants have taken. Amicable settlement

---

[2] Pfeiffer, R. H., *Introduction to the Old Testament,* p. 150. New York: Harper & Brothers, 1941.

of the issue establishes the reliability of kindness and understanding as a way of living well with others. In other words, one starts out to learn by trial and error, then through the accumulation of experiences of better and worse arrives at principles which have general bearing upon conduct for future occasions.

It should be emphasized that respect does not flow automatically from acts of kindness. Sometimes the opposite result appears. It is only when kindness is linked with strength that it becomes effective. In the negotiations for the cave of Machpelah as a burying place Ephron, the Hittite owner, offers to give the land to Abram. Bowing low in gracious acknowledgment, the patriarch counters the neighbor's generosity by insisting on paying for it and weighs out four hundred shekels of silver in the value of standards current in the country. The ancient customs governing such exchanges do not obscure the genuine respect that lies at the center of the transaction. The inward sense of self-worth, key to all sound relations with others, means far more than capacity to pay. It keeps the balance that refuses to exploit or to be exploited. What happens when this element of character is lacking or suppressed is clearly evident in the behavior of Isaac. Although the picture of him in the traditions is vague, the impression of his easygoing benevolence is unmistakable. When again dispute arises over the wells in the valley of Gerar, Isaac solves the problem by withdrawing instead of standing his ground as his father had done. "The Lord has made room for us" is the way he explains his action. It is this mood of passivity that later compromises his position in his own house. Kindness that is associated with inner weakness comes up short in the end. When joined with strength in treating another as one's own kind, it can seal the bonds of sound human relations. Then it is supported by respect.

The winning of self-respect out of interaction with other people is the first great achievement of the soul. It is the beginning of real self-consciousness whose first stage is commonly designated as individuality with components of self-awareness and self-acceptance. At this time, the soul takes its place at the center of a universe of expanding relationships, issues its claims, defines its obligations, and construes its destiny.

It is far from accidental that this internal event should be closely associated with sex, uniting at once the fact of differentiation from others and inevitable linkage with them. The biological basis of the inner life is inescapable, for it engages the joint issue of self-fulfillment and self-transcendence. No fact is more explicitly recognized in the Old Testament than this. The place of sex is taken for granted, treated openly and frankly, and at times, to a sensitive mind, shockingly.[3] It is inept to defend or explain these attitudes by reference to their appearance in a special "primitive" age when, as a matter of fact, the primitive survives in every age, conditions every human individual, and is probably nowhere more manifest than in the sexual preoccupations of modern minds. In the story of Israel, sex is viewed with realism and

---

[3] Genesis 38. (RSV)

reverence, all aberrations to the contrary notwithstanding. It is appropriately taken as the mark of racial distinction in the rite of circumcision and works itself out directly in Abram's concern first for a son, and then in the choice of a wife for him when Providence grants him one. The deep emotions and strong romantic sentiments so sensitively portrayed in the negotiations for Rebekah are wholesome and valid evidence of the meaning of sex in the history of the soul and reveal its satisfaction in being true to itself. Fuller implications of these basic facts appear in the changing settings of later development. It is already clear, however, that sex is integral to human nature on all levels of experience. It is soundly associated with self-respect in Israel and directly related, even there, to the cultural and spiritual adventure of mankind.[4]

Once the soul achieves sufficient internal organization to become aware of its own unique qualities with an intensified feeling of difference from others, there is an increased sensitivity to the risks of interaction with the external world. Everywhere there are threats to integrity, and at times the temptation to put on the mask of appearance not matched by inward character is very strong. The destruction of Sodom and Gomorrah has the effect of a traumatic event in the experience of Abram. The depth of his involvement in the evils of the world through his kinsman's association

---

[4] Following Pfeiffer's analysis of the documents in Genesis, it is significant to note that the more perverse sexual episodes, as well as the story of the Fall, come from a pessimistic source alien in spirit to the predominant mood of the Jahwist and Elohist traditions.

with the cities is revealed in the long and persistent inter-
cession for him. Lot's escape by a hair's breadth serves notice on the soul that its journey through the world is
marked by the presence of forces which at any moment may
overwhelm it. Wickedness, the term which describes behavior alien to one's own dedicated purpose, is subtle and attractive, inviting one to dissipate the very powers needed to
attain self-fulfillment. Rejection of the appeal of evil must
be drastic and complete. The decision required is set forth
in the dramatic result of the backward look of Lot's wife
after she has been barely extricated from the doomed cities.

It is in the presence of such scenes as this that the soul,
bearing its burden of autonomy, seeks reassurance. This is
an outstanding feature of the story of Abram. Repeatedly
in times of doubt and crisis the promise returns in unequivocal affirmation. "I will bless thee and make thee
great." "Fear not, I am thy shield and thy exceeding great
reward." These words recur almost like the refrain of a
hymn. The climax is reached when the new name bearing
approval of individuality and guarantees for the future is
given: "Thy name shall be Abraham, for a father of many
nations I have made thee." Associated with this feeling that
one is on the right road, is a growing conviction that one
need not yield to forces in the immediate environment that
are incompatible with one's purposes. There are resources
for the inner life over which the neighbors have no control
and they are directly available for appropriation in terms
of the distinctive mission one must fulfill. One can shape

the world he wishes to live in by decisions that have
origin in a Will which is wiser than one's own and
which the neighbors have no ultimate power.

In one of the later additions to the patriarchal tradition,
there is dramatic emphasis upon growth in self-confidence
and the unique capacity of the soul to rest its destiny upon
the fortunes of faith. Abraham's response to the command
to sacrifice Isaac, only son and heir to the promise, expresses
more than Israel's aversion to human sacrifice. It discloses
that quality of the soul which we call courage, or the capacity steadily to pursue one's course in the face of critical
circumstances without knowing what the outcome is going
to be. The belief that "the Lord sees" or "will provide,"
that in spite of all that appears capricious and hidden there
is a basic reliability in the order of the world, is the second
signal accomplishment of the early years. It is self-consciousness integrating self-respect with trust, affirming that life is
worth while, and that the release of one's powers in decision
and action related to a worthy goal is an all-absorbing adventure.

2. *Bargaining with the World*

In the next stage of its development, the soul enters a new
setting where individuality asserts itself in seeking the conquest of the external world through the acquisition of possessions. This is the main feature of events in the house of
Isaac where, with pervasive humor and remarkable insight
into human motivation, the essential elements of family

interaction are described.[5] Some factors ordinarily operating unconsciously in the shaping of personality are boldly
acted out. Two sons, Esau and Jacob, contend with each
other from the first. The background of their rivalry is
plainly reflected in the preferences of the parents each of
whom behaves according to character—Isaac the only son of
Abraham by Sarah, and Rebekah the resourceful woman
who, without deviating from her essential role, knows what
she wants and how to get it. Their favoritism with respect
to the children has an equivocal basis in view of the fact
that the boys are twins and the question of their relative
ages could be easily argued.

A choice in line with destiny has to be made, and it is
the mother who judges the fitness of the lads for leadership.
In the presence of the passive Isaac who is pictured here as
a pale figure in the seat of patriarchal prerogative, she is
the agent of decision. She appraises the traits of Esau and
lays her plan in the pattern of the bond between him and
his father. Jacob responds readily to her training and acts
according to her dictates. With some semblance of openness
in the matter, he secures Esau's relinquishment of his right
as first-born in exchange for a bowl of lentil soup. If this
seems a pittance for so much, the margin of seniority between the two is likewise only a matter of a very short time.
But for a brief interval, Jacob would stand in the right
legal shoes of primogeniture. His words to his father are a

---

[5] Genesis 25:21-35; 29. (RSV) As an example of intrafamily rivalries,
this story anticipates in a remarkable way the oedipal situation of
which Sigmund Freud made so much.

bare-faced lie, but some of the force is taken out of it by the fact that the old man, for all his passivity and blindness, seems to know what he is doing. Again the situation is equivocal—"the hands of Esau" and "the voice of Jacob."

This is really the way the situation stands so far as the blessing is concerned. If the issue is between twins, should not the abler be chosen as first and the other justly accorded his due in second place? After all, in Hebrew logic, does not priority belong to him whose capacity is equal to the task? At any rate, Rebekah's intuitions and skill are adequate for the occasion and Jacob presses his advantage while the situation regarding Esau is not left without remedy. In this stage, the soul passes from the period of random wandering and becomes planful and subtle in preparation for moving on to the mastery of a settled way of life. Initial accomplishment in competition with others gives rise to a conceit about one's importance, but this undergoes change when privileged position issues in corresponding duties.

Once the blessing is bestowed, it must take its course in determining future events. Both parents play their part in Jacob's departure. One emphasizes the serious business of seeking a wife in the land of his ancestors; the other prods the fledgling from the nest by pointing to the anger of the dispossessed brother. Apron strings are snipped without flinching. The time is at hand for manhood to assert itself. Childhood ambition clothed in the glamor of a daydream nurtured in Rebekah's tent must come to terms with reality. The scene at Bethel, first stop on the way to Paddan-aram, presents a true adolescent crisis. The stone, a cult object, on which Jacob lays his head as night comes on, is the symbol of inward groping for security and guidance. It is an awesome moment mingling dread with search and hope. When the vision comes, it brings the voice of history reaffirming the promise to the fathers and imposing the burden of keeping faith with the past by maintaining integrity in decision and performance. Such responsibility adds another dimension to the soul.

In practice, the principle of being true to oneself is subject to two demands which, under normal conditions, are always in a state of tension. On the one hand, there is the inward conviction derived from meanings which flow from an ultimate objective commanding the highest devotion and loyalty. On the other, there is the necessity of acting in the immediate, concrete situation where the connection with this purpose is often obscure and where, indeed, the purpose may be compromised at many points, or not served at all. The soul is constantly faced with the odds of better and worse in relating these demands to each other. In the case of Jacob, they are acted out without concealment or sophisticated inhibition. In him, human nature, after the manner characteristic of the Old Testament, stalks right out into broad daylight and exposes itself, without parade, for what it really is. In the house of Laban, he continues true to his prototype as usurper. He accepts the terms of marriage as they are set before him and exploits his extended tenure for the maximum of profit. For a time, it is nip and tuck as he matches wits with his kinsman who grudgingly admits that the relationship is not without its advantages to him.

But things gradually get out of balance, and after the affair of the breeding of the flocks at the watering troughs, the die of separation is cast. Jacob secretly prepares to make off with his gains—wives, concubines, slaves, flocks, and other portable wealth. He justifies the decision to his wives in terms of the noble call of independence and destiny. When pursued and overtaken by Laban, his defense is ready. He has labored twenty years under changing contract. He has taken losses from the flocks incurred by attacks of wild beasts. He has endured the heat of the Syrian sun by day, the cold by night, accompanied by frequent occasions of sleeplessness. He has suffered the humiliation of a change of wages ten times. With these facts properly rationalized, he makes a convincing case supported not a little by Laban's remorse for his own misdeeds. When it is declared that the results correspond to divine intention, there is no room for further argument. The gods of both parties are called to witness an oath taken in pledge of mutual toleration. For Jacob, however, a further settlement remains.

The soul continues to learn by experience, but it carries with it a record involving consequences that cannot be dismissed. Self-consciousness, though now invested with the prestige of worldly goods, must face the judgment of the meeting with Esau and the expiation of guilt in offerings and reconciliation. On the borders of Canaan the final issue is joined. All that has gone before comes to new focus in the struggle by the brook Jabbok. It is in this context of forces within itself, environed by external threat, that the soul attains the victory of insight into its nature and destiny. The new name sets the pattern of the future—"Israel." The episode ends with the meeting of the estranged brother, the proffer of rich gifts, Esau's gracious declination with words of forgiveness that contain a strange mockery of the old days of rivalry back home. "I have enough, my brother; keep that thou hast for thyself." But the gifts are accepted, and the soul is again in balance. The final event comes in the reaffirmation of distinctiveness as Jacob enters Canaan and insists on the circumcision of the sons of Hamor at Shechem as the condition of marriage with his daughters. The old vows are renewed at Bethel and the shrine consecrated El-Bethel, a name more in accord with his further engagement with history.

3. *The Drive for Power*

In the remarkable unveiling of the inner life set forth in the Joseph stories, the third dimension of self-consciousness appears in the drive for power.[6] Here again the artistry of the writers moves with penetrating and colorful insight through a succession of events in which the soul exults in dominion over others. The setting is fully furnished with all the elements which the picture requires. Jacob's attachment to Joseph, first-born of the beloved Rachel, his pref-

---

[6] Genesis 37:1-48:14. (RSV)

erence openly expressed in the family relationships, the
lad's strong identification with his father, nurtured by close
association and indulgent favor, are all a bright boy needs
to incite him to thoughts of extraordinary achievements.
The dreams stake out his claims, and there is no restraint
in communicating them to those directly affected by them.
His ascendancy over the household is to be supreme.

Even more is implied. The dream of the sheaves in the
field is the witness of earth while the other involving the
sun, moon, and stars attests the decree of heaven. It is in
the perspective of both that the soul takes its bearings, the
one disclosing the immediate field of action, the other
pointing toward remote but assured boundaries beyond the
reach of sight. The dreams, therefore, are not merely a
trivial "hunch" from the depths but, in the Hebrew conception of them, a declaration that what they say must
become fact and that the dreamer has in himself the power
to actualize them.[7] The anger of the brothers is accentuated
by their realization of these implications—to them, of
course, preposterous arrogance. Jacob's rebuke of Joseph
for such avowal of ambition is tempered by the fact that
"he kept the saying in mind." It is evident that he is on the
side of the dreams. They conform to his bias, and he knows
that the outcome which they predict is inevitable. Subsequent events follow from this premonitory incident. Human nature takes its course on both sides of the issue. The
brothers conspire against Joseph, are divided at first in their

---

[7] Pedersen, Johannes, *Israel—Its Life and Culture*, I-II, pp. 136, 137.
London: Oxford University Press, 1926.

counsel concerning the proper disposition of him, and finally sell him to the Ishmaelites, descendants of the outcast Hagar.

The measure of strength in the soul becomes manifest in the resistance of forces arrayed against it in the external world. Aggressive self-assertion alternates with submission to opposition which, for the moment, cannot be overcome. Soul force is mainly a matter of inner certitude supported by the kind of integration which gives control over the powers at one's command, deploys them as occasion requires, and restrains them altogether when action would be fruitless. Self-command is the essence of command over others.

All these qualities emerge in Joseph. The power of the dream continues in Egypt. It works quietly and effectively behind the mask of the slave in the house of Potiphar. It conserves virility in the face of seduction. Falsely accused, it meets the fate of imprisonment and wins honor there. Basic integrity is not compromised by change of roles; it impresses its character on everything it touches. In the career of Joseph, the soul is fully aware of this power. It makes terms with the butler and the baker, and in the interpretation of their dreams subtly announces its jurisdiction over life and death. In the quest for mastery, alternatives presented by the external world are carefully weighed and action chosen in the light of probabilities ahead. For these, the soul must have the strength to wait. When the dreams of Pharaoh do not yield to the divining wit of his magicians, the butler's faulty memory improves and Joseph is ushered into the presence of the monarch. Here, writ large with compelling detail, the soul of the disciplined shepherd—self-conscious in its integrity and mission—confronts supreme worldly power, panoplied in all its attributes, and exacts tribute from it. The king's dreams are drawn to the measure of Joseph's inner stature. They portend national disaster on a devastating scale. Joseph's discernment of the nature and certainty of the event and his spontaneous counsel for saving the country are, by reason of their union in him, equivalent to self-elevation to office. Pharaoh's appointment of him confirms established competence. The office carries with it all the external signs of the internal state of the soul—the signet ring, royal robes, the second chariot, a new name, and popular acknowledgment by all the people bowing the knee. Marriage to the daughter of the priest of On adds strength to the linkage with royalty and completes the naturalization of Joseph in the seat of authority in Egypt.

The power of the soul, however, is not fully established by exercising the ability to get what it wants through seizing opportunity and manipulating circumstances. This alone would be aggrandizement which in the end corrupts purpose and dissipates inward strength. The will to take must be balanced by the will to give. Beneficence is also a way to rule. The visits of the dependent brothers present in impressive scenes the humor and seriousness of the great reversal and lay out unmistakably the power that was there in the beginning. The acts of generosity are accompanied by a humiliation that is carried out with the utmost premeditation and calculation. Joseph calls them "spies," embarrasses them by secretly putting their money in their sacks and demanding hostage for Benjamin's appearance at his court. When the latter arrives, he is made the victim of the pretended theft of the royal cup while the threat of holding him for the crime adds the inconsolable grief of their aged father to the anguish of the brothers. In bestowing his bounty, Joseph exacts the tribute of the most moving emotions designed to purge them of their guilt and reduce them to helpless waiting on his will. Momentarily the soul exults in its advantage as the drama moves toward a climax which, in actuality, surpasses the intimations of the dreams.

In all this behavior on the part of Joseph the main motif continues its work in the weeping which parallels the despair of the brothers and prepares the way for the disclosure of his identity. When this takes place, the whole scene is suffused by a sense of solidarity in both the evil done and the good that now overcomes it. The reunion with Jacob and the assignment of the clans to a region appropriate to their occupation as shepherds completes the work of beneficence, and the soul is at peace with itself. The drive for power, restrained only by an unseen Presence, attains supremacy in Joseph's final official acts establishing the absolute sovereignty of Pharaoh over Egypt. This outcome of involvement with the world declares, by the majesty of external event, the inward strength which enables the soul of Israel to march on into history.

4. *Conscience*

The fourth dimension of self-consciousness is conscience. This is the significance of Moses who stands at the summit of Israel's achievement in the early years.[8] To that we must now address ourselves.

There are few pages in the Old Testament that stir the imagination more than the opening chapters of the Book of Exodus. With a few swift strokes, the scene of a momentous event in the history of the soul is presented. Three facts set the stage for the action which ensues—the coming to the throne of Egypt of a king "who knew not Joseph," the threat of the Hebrews to the Egyptians by virtue of their increasing numbers, and the adoption of a drastic policy to deal with the problem. Again there is to be a contest of power, but the circumstances are shaped to a different ordering of events. Joseph attained his ends by manipulating Pharaoh from his own position as second in authority. The new situation requires an organized, mass revolt of a whole people, and a kind of deliverance that will be conclusive proof of the uniqueness of Israel, an event to be held in everlasting remembrance as incentive for sustained loyalty to inherent genius. It is a crisis greater than any that has gone before offering alternatives of creative advance toward higher attainment or regression through absorption by an alien people. The choice is between slavery and full autonomy in freedom.

---

[8] Exodus 1-24.

We do not read far into the record before it becomes clear that this is to be creation. The principal symbols which ancient man used to present to himself the origin of the world are there—water, fire (light, lightning), and the mountain. In suspense we follow the inviting little story of the threat to the baby, the mother's shrewdness in setting him adrift in the river with his sister on guard, the coming of the princess to bathe, his temporary placement with his mother, and his adoption by the princess. It is immeasurable innocence cloaking a mighty act. The words of the princess in naming the child, "Moses, because I drew him out of the water," are reminiscent of primeval beginnings preserved in eastern lore extending even unto China. Water is the original chaos out of which the earth and life came.

Quickly the story moves to the day when the grown-up Moses looks upon the burdens of his people and the issue is sharpened by the sight of an Egyptian striking a Hebrew. He slays the Egyptian and buries his body in the sand. The next day he encounters two Hebrews struggling together and questions the aggressor. The reply which he receives indicates that his act of the previous day is known, and he flees from the country. In these five brief verses the whole issue of right and wrong in human relations is set forth. The Egyptian oppression of the Hebrews is reduced to a combat between two men representing both groups. The contest between the Hebrews is of a different order, two members of the same race, but it focuses on the same kind of conduct. Taken together, the two incidents present the fact of the universality of right and wrong and the rele-

vance of moral judgment to every man in his dealings with
his fellow men. In his response to the lashing of the Hebrew, Moses seeks redress of wrong by direct action. In the
second case, that method is challenged—"Who made you a
prince and a judge over us?" He runs for his life, but the
question causes him to react to his own deed in terms of a
wider context of reality. Does not the wrong of the Egyptian oppression express the corporate act of a whole people? Is not the plight of the Hebrews set in a similar pattern? Are not all men bound up in the bundle of life?
Appraised in this light, it is clear that individual action,
abetted by anger, offers no adequate solution, though the
fact remains that individual judgment is indispensable as
preparation for any kind of appropriate action.

The incident of the burning bush in Midian leads directly to the inner battleground where the soul seeks to
resolve the conflict in itself in order that it may serve the
solution required by the conflict between men in the external world. It is in Moses' anger, the flaming indignation
that burns but does not consume, that we see the stuff out
of which conscience is made. Later this becomes more explicit in the abounding energy of Horeb where surging,
primitive emotions are reflected in the lightning and thun-
der over the mountain. The awe of diffused power, from an
unseen source, subdues the people and compels their acceptance of discipline. The fortunes of the soul are wrought
out in the presence of forces which, on the one hand,
threaten to destroy it and, on the other, invite it to ordered
conduct which supports a higher destiny. Such a place in

man's earthly journey is indeed ground on which one would tread with care, shuddering before destruction at the moment of new creation. The occasion calls for brooding inward search and planning in the measure of the task at hand.

It is no accident that the anxiety of Moses should center in his ineptitude for speech, for words are the chief weapons of the soul and this is to be a battle of attrition in which inward, articulate judgment will subdue the opposition. It is the power of right against wrong that is to be demonstrated. This is the objective of the scenes where the might of Egypt is arrayed on the one side and only a voice on the other. The hardened heart of Pharaoh accentuates the inward nature of the conflict and the account of the plagues is a masterpiece in the drama of calculated assault upon wrong, insistently urging, "Let my people go." Deliverance comes not by armies but by "strength of hand"; not by arbitrary decree, but by words announcing the claims of justice. This is the power of conscience mobilizing resources for penetrating the inner seat of decision and winning a verdict that satisfies the demand for balance and integrity in human relations.

Thus we are led to the final issue of the early years. Looking back along the path which we have followed, what do we see? First of all, a tendency continuously operative in the soul, implicit in the account already given, must be mentioned. This activity of the internal life may be called by different names, but the most appropriate designation from the standpoint of our context is recapitulation, or the tendency of the soul to relive its past in the present and to modify that past through response to current demands and projected possibilities of the future.[9]

This does not mean that in being true to itself the soul follows a pattern of mere repetition. On the contrary, as we have clearly seen, integrity involves living in the fullness of all one's potentialities. This is accomplished by bringing the past into new settings out of which further internal development flows. Each of the components of self-consciousness stands apart in our analysis because they are respectively at the center of the situations where action takes place. All of them—individuality, the need for security and status provided by possessions, the drive for power, and so on—are found together in some degree in all the settings, for the reason that they must collaborate wherever human behavior appears. Our separation of them, warranted by a core of central emphasis in the stories, serves the interest of contributing insight to our understanding of human

---

[9] Recapitulation as an aspect of human behavior is found outside of the biblical material we have been studying. For example, in examining some archeological artifacts, two pieces of pottery, parts of jars with handles, were noted. In one, estimated to have been used in the time of David about the year one thousand B.C., the handle was plain and rounded like a sturdy circle. In the other, dated the eighth or seventh century B.C., there were two differences. The handle was flattened to allow the insertion of the four fingers on the inside and the clasping of the thumb on the outside to complete the grasp of the hand. There was also clear evidence of ribbing to keep the hand from slipping, or perchance to add a touch of ornamentation. Thus we see that in the fashioning of the later handle, the process of the earlier was recapitulated with additions. Other illustrations support the view that this is one of the common ways in which human creativity manifests itself.

nature. The names of "Abraham, Isaac, and Jacob," so often repeated together in the Bible, to which we add the names of Joseph and Moses, stand for a whole of self-consciousness whose constituent elements are revealed in concrete situations adorned with rich detail and essential accuracy. Recoded in our prosaic, occidental categories, the inner life is what these stories say it is.

Towering above all is conscience. Intimations of it appear in the earliest traditions but none deals directly with it until we come to Moses. There it attains the peak of formulation and action. Its importance in human nature cannot be overemphasized. With due respect to the Greeks, it must be said that conscience, in the Hebrew conception of it, is greater than reason. Indeed, its task is to rule reason. Its focus is on the values governing human relations. It uses reason to analyze the values, to lay them out in perspective, so to speak, but it is not to be equated to reason itself. Conscience is judge. As its name implies, it is the seat of power in the soul where knowledge gained from a wide variety of experiences is brought together and united in the execution of an act called "right." But this internal ordering of the values of life must be projected outward in a social organization that tests their vitality and validity, and provides the basis for further human advance. In other words, ultimately the inward rule of conscience is translated into law to organize freedom in social relations by setting bounds to excesses of individual action. When, however, such organization becomes rigid, burdensome, and too restrictive of individual growth, the soul must again, through conscience, mobilize its resources for reformation. The relations between the internal and the external orders at any time are reciprocal; but the creative center, the source of insight and change, is in the internal life.

In concluding this chapter, we must look back upon the course we have followed for the purpose of discovering what has come to light concerning the issues which are before us in this study. We have spoken of the soul as the total animate creature and observed its behavior in the form given to it by early Hebrew man. We shall continue to use the term in this sense, both with respect to the individual and to the corporate life of Israel. But, in order to differentiate those elements which distinguish man from the animals and account for the religious character of the human adventure, we need now to go as far as our data will allow in making a more pointed and analytic examination of the internal life. Within these bounds, what are the components of the soul?

First, there is the biosocial self. What is its character? It exists in a living body which, though intricately designed and finely balanced within the structure of nature, is subject to the perils of hunger, disease, and death. The tomb in Haran, on the edge of a desert, is motive for migration toward green pastures and flowing waters. Physical sustenance must be drawn from the breast of the good earth, from field and flock and herd. Security, in all that the word conveys, is basic in any scheme of life. At the minimum, it requires ready access to nature's resources without cessation of flow from supply to consumer. Defenses must be built against scarcity and misfortune arising from error in calculation or unforeseen catastrophe. But this is not all. He who seeks better opportunity in a new place will be almost certain to find others occupying the land. One must manage to survive under competition. Means are available for doing this. In the nature of being a biosocial self, one can anticipate how the neighbors feel about their own need and what they want beyond that. This ability to take the role of another, inwardly to perceive his point of view, enables one to learn the art of placing restraint upon oneself, of bargaining for advantage, and tolerating the peculiarities of other people. Abraham's capacity to induce respect and to confer benefit upon his rivals makes it possible for him to enter into agreements that add to his security. But the tensions of competition are not usually resolved once for all. There are needs which extend beyond economics. Desire for status and prestige may press the claim for power over others and result in seizure of position as a supreme self among other selves. Coercion, compromise, subtle wit, and kindness are some of the options from which one may choose. As a self, one can, with the support of nature, affirm an individuality having the right to amass possessions at another's expense. A sense of cause and proper opportunity may command the destiny of a Pharaoh. To mitigate extremes and establish a more settled order in human relations, conscience may be called to sit in judgment on right and wrong and mediate the ways of men to one another. These are some typical traits of the biosocial self. If, however, this were all that belonged to the soul, the philosophy of its working in the world would be hardly more than a canny and sophisticated prudence. Self-preservation of a cultural animal would almost sum up the matter.

Far more conspicuous and decisive in the constitution and behavior of the soul of Israel is the conviction that human living involves much more than being an effective self among other selves. From the beginning, Hebrew man acts under command of a higher Power. Abraham receives his commission from God. He feels subject to a directive that presides over history, external to himself yet answering to an inner need not satisfied in social experience. His consultations with God, his repeated return to altars of prayer under the open sky for renewal and recovery of perspective, his courage to take risks beyond the counsels of prudence express faith in a purpose that transcends mere competence to get along in the world. Likewise Jacob's wrestling at the ford of the Jabbok, Joseph's dreams uniting immediate action with ultimate sanction, the call of Moses in Midian, and other events we have mentioned make clear beyond doubt the search of the soul for affiliation with the divine. What the patriarchs conceive to be their destiny is, of course, served by the biosocial self through its procreative capacity and the shaping of a social order through which the rule of Yahweh is to be manifest in the earth. Although this rule in many situations is almost identical with the aspirations of the biosocial self, early tradition carries the germ of self-transcendence in the idea that through Israel special blessing will come to the world. Biosocial man is already expressing himself as be-

lieving man, a trait which will produce important consequences in later pages of this book.

Thus it turns out that although conscience stands at the
peak of the biosocial self, it cannot be trusted as final ar-
biter in the adventure of man. Indeed, to give it ascendancy
would falsify the reality of the larger setting in which the
soul has its existence. Human values arranged in some sort
of hierarchy come tumbling down of their own weight, as
did the ancient empires surrounding Israel, unless they are
sustained by a Power greater than conscience and whose
presence is discerned in the ordering of the universe that
is not man. Without the constant reassurance which came
to Moses from "I am that I am" (Yahweh), the adventure
which he led into the wilderness would have come to
naught as a lost cause. The spirit of his dedication and the
solidarity of Israel in the covenant of the divine purpose is
expressed in one of the last prayers attributed to him,
"Pardon our iniquity and take us for thine inheritance."

It is this courageous and imaginative quality of the soul
of Israel, manifest in the early years and sustained in earnest search for fulfillment transcending mere human attainment, that lays the foundation of enduring monument
destined to inspire the Nation's further adventure and, ultimately, to shape the moral character of western man.

2. THE MIDDLE YEARS

MODERN PSYCHOLOGY ATTEMPTS TO EXAMINE the soul as an object in nature. It seeks understanding of man by adapting the methods of natural science to the peculiar requirements of this task and invents categories or concepts which can be organized in some sort of system. Its procedures are descriptive and analytic, and its results are articulated inferences from behavior. The point of observation is the engagement of the human organism with its environment in progressive adaptations which move from intra-uterine gestation to adulthood. Great importance is attached to the socialization of the infant, its incorporation of the attitudes of parents and siblings, and the effect of these influences upon subsequent development. It is presumed that all later experiences are assimilated to the patterns laid down in the early years. In this process, the human body is considered to be primary. It is the medium of social interaction registering, retaining, and organizing responses to the external world. The "soul" as the inner unity of these reactions is inseparable from the physical surrounding which nurtures and limits it. On occasion it appears free to search out new ways of adjustment, but ultimately it yields to the demands of the structure within which it must find comfort in accommodation and release.

It is instructive to compare this formal orientation of psychology with the Bible whose subject is also the nature of the soul in its search for integration and fulfillment. Viewing the literature as a whole, it is possible to mark parallels between these two accounts of human nature by recognizing that a race has its infancy, its childhood, adolescence, adulthood, and old age. The specifics of these stages in the history of a people cannot be translated directly into terms that conform to the life of an individual. But in so far as these steps are identifiable by generalized and characteristic attitudes, the comparison gains force. The Bible is not a study of the soul as an object in nature. It is an autobiography of the soul. Like all autobiography, the story cannot begin until the age of self-consciousness is reached and the people chosen for this service to mankind have attained sufficient maturity of insight to look back upon and examine the meaning of their adventure. The writers of this history are acutely aware of the limitations which the human body places upon the soul in its earthly journey, but they make no attempt to give us a treatise on physiology or to discuss the subtleties of the relations of body and mind in the modern manner. Their concern is with man as an autonomous being in actual engagement with time and circumstance. The basic pattern of this life, as we have seen, is laid down in the early years and is marked by its direct and intimate dependence upon its Creator. Differentiation from the world and other men, instituted by the act of creation itself, shows that variety of random impulse, primitive organization and movement associated with infancy and childhood.

The next period, which we are about to examine, discloses increasing self-assertion of the soul, its search for a place among peers, its responsiveness to their ways—hesitating, judging and choosing among them—and its deliberate effort to establish a secure position in history. This is the essential significance of the middle years as we are thinking of them in relation to Israel as prototype of the internal life of man.

The history presented in Numbers and Joshua continues the account of events which Moses initiated in the wilderness in completing the organization of the tribes for the entrance into the land of Canaan. His strong hand, his patience, his capacity for maintaining order and discipline bear fruit after many years, and the children of Israel enter the land promised to their fathers. The laws of the covenant, expressing the inner perception of Moses concerning an ordered life that would preserve the genius of Israel and advance it toward higher fulfillment, become the basis of the future history. The story of the settlement in Canaan, systematized in the Book of Joshua and somewhat idealized, presents the essentials regarding the division of the land and the work of completing the conquest. That all does not go well is clear. Difficulties of living among people already in possession of the land and capable of resistance appear on almost every page of the record. The course of events ebbs and flows as the Book of Judges indicates. Nevertheless, the soul of Israel, secure in the promise to Abraham, remains intact; and each occasion in the setting of better and worse produces leadership that holds the ground gained in anticipation of a brighter future beyond.

In the time of Samuel, it becomes apparent that more sustained attempt at consolidation of the interests of the people must be undertaken. Although the account of deterioration in the house of Eli may be exaggerated, it is clear that the slackening, if not corruption, of religious loyalty calls for remedy. To this internal condition is added the continuous encroachment of external enemies, now concentrated in the Philistine menace, the most threatening of all the neighbors. It was at this juncture of events that the demand for a monarchy arose. Like the record of the early years, the history of this period, drawn from differing sources, is repetitious and confused at many points, but the composite left by the redactors is adequate for an examination of the internal state of Israel during the age of developing nationalism.

In this part of our task, as in the study of the previous period, we shall allow the record to speak for itself. But it will be in point to discern that the monarchy presents a new phase of the inward contest between the components of the soul of Israel previously mentioned. The biosocial self, now assuming the character of a nation bent on making its position secure among other corporate selves, continues in tension with the demands of an objective transcending self. The simpler agreements of the former time, reached in limited face-to-face situations and adequate for governing human relations under the sanctions of conscience, are now superseded by measures more in accord with the new conditions. Free and open bargaining, compromise, and mutual exchanges of benefit between tribal chiefs no longer suffice. Defense, a primary right of the self, must be implemented by political organization to guarantee internal cohesion, and by military force to express the will to live among competitors, perchance to attain superiority and domination over them.

The behavior which appears in this setting rather temptingly invites a more technical use of current psychology, but we are deliberately reserving this form of interpretation for a more appropriate occasion and a more pertinent context of fact. It is enough to say here that the age of the kings in Israel is marked by a kind of response which the challenge of external enemies requires and is calculated in terms of the methods which the enemy uses. To hold at bay, or to conquer, by force is the aim. Pursuing this course, the history discloses four major stages. There is first the period of wavering self-confidence and uncertain weighing of issues in the time of Saul. This is followed by an increasing sense of unity and power which is qualified by an epidemic of internal rivalries. Then comes Solomon and the period of temporary supremacy. After this, decline and a house divided against itself. In these events, we shall see human nature acting out its impulses, shaping purposes amidst jealousies and variant ambitions, sometimes with brilliance and courage, sometimes with vacillation ending in grief, often with vengeance and brutality. The whole, to us, will be a living parable of man's effort to find out who he is in the tumult of forces that stir him to thought and action.

In all this, one crucial fact must not be overlooked. By the experiences of this period, it will become clearer that the soul of Israel is being shaped by a kind of reaction to failure that is not found in similar character in any other ancient people. Disappointment and defeat in the ventures of the self become causes for deeper scrutiny of its nature and its need for salvation. The human adventure is seen to be under the sovereignty of a higher Power, Yahweh, who acts from the outside and who uses the failures of self as a discipline for making His rule within the soul supreme. In this fact, we shall discover the relevance of our data for the nurture of religious living and seek, as a part of that end, a thorough grounding of pastoral theology in the Bible. We turn now to the middle years for their contribution to this purpose.

1. *Theocracy Falters in Armor*

When the elders of Israel consult Samuel with regard to a king, he resists the proposal.[1] Advocate of the early faith, he

---

[1] I Samuel 8, 9. In the beginning, the Hebrew conception of the kingship seems to have possessed a character somewhat similar to that in other cultures of the Near East at the time. It was invested with attributes of the deity. Coronation ceremonies expressed this relationship. The king could officiate as priest, and was regarded as the protector of fertility and prosperity.

points out what it will mean to have a ruler whose duties may divert him and the people from loyalty to the inner purpose which was confirmed by the deliverance from Egypt. The soul knows that there is threat in the step which it must take, but each issue must be met where it appears, always in the concrete situation where decision is to be made and action taken. For the soul, there can be no sheer, abstract aloofness from the world. The people need security in their daily living. They seek self-preservation and opportunity to advance their interests. "We will have a king" that "we may be like other nations," equal to them and adequate for the threat which they present to us, a king who will fight our battles for us. Samuel yields to the force of the argument.

The candidate for the new office first appears in a rather unobtrusive way on a mission to find his father's asses which are lost. His name is Saul, a Benjamite, son of Kish. Unsuccessful in finding the objects of his search, his servant suggests that they consult a seer who will be able to help them. In this way Saul arrives at the house of Samuel in Ramah. In external appearance, he has the marks of the kind of leader Israel needs. He is handsome, physically large, of heroic build, head and shoulders above any man of the tribes with a bearing to inspire confidence in friend and incite fear in foe. Impressed that this is the man, Samuel takes him into the house for the night, and on the morrow anoints him and sends him away after telling him the signs by which he shall know that he is king. The anointing is more than a form. It is induction into an office for which a man is given "another heart" endowing him with powers commensurate with responsibilities. The office unites king, people, and destiny. In this act, there is presumptive hope that high purpose will be served.

In presenting Saul to the people, Samuel takes care to make explicit the opportunities and dangers involved in the new step.[2] It is clear that the self-realization of the soul of Israel depends on the way it behaves in the new setting of circumstances and its capacity to shape them to ends approved by historic mission. One called to serve such a purpose in behalf of his people might well be filled with awe, but this is not the meaning of Saul's hiding in the baggage at the moment when he is to be installed as king.[3] There is more than a hint of doubt concerning the qualifications of the man who has been chosen. Indeed, on the side, dissident voices are saying, "How can this man save us?" Nevertheless, when he is brought out, the people shout, "Long live the king!" The doubt subsides when Saul meets the initial test in the field against the Ammonites. He musters strength to respond to the challenge, and the result increases the people's confidence in him. Samuel's rehearsal of the past of Israel and his counsel regarding the conditions upon which continued success is predicated seal the fate of king and people in their mutual obligations. The kingship has evil in it, but an unhappy outcome may be averted if there is no turning aside for vain undertakings, no compromising with inner integrity.

---

[2] I Samuel 10:25f; 12:6-25.

[3] I Samuel 10:20-27.

In the Philistine assaults, the troops tremble behind Saul
who, in spite of all the questioning about him, manifests
genuine desire to serve his people well. But he blunders
in the difficult task of uniting the claims made upon him
as a general in the field with the religious solemnity of his
office. He takes matters in his own hands in the sacrifices
at Gilgal after waiting seven days for Samuel.[4] It is a case
of military necessity, as we would say, but on the premises
set forth, the action is presumptuous and improper. Thus
to the weakness of a poorly equipped army, Saul adds rash-
ness and insensitivity to the deeper significance of the work
to which he has been called. In the role of King of Israel,
the soul is awkward in its self-consciousness with qualities
not unlike the adolescent who is eager and sincere in the
wish to succeed but unsure of himself. In a similar manner,
Saul foolishly issues a command that no food shall be eaten
until evening and the Philistines are vanquished in the
final engagement at Michmash. The curse of death is placed
upon anyone who disobeys the order.

In his own house, however, there is a different kind of
courage ready to act independently and win honors for
itself. Jonathan and his armor bearer make a singlehanded
entry into the camp of the enemy. Unaware of his father's
decree, he takes food during the day and becomes subject
to the prescribed penalty. When he is confronted with the
implications of his deed, he exposes the bad logic of the
King in imposing a restriction that reduced the efficiency

---

[4] I Samuel 13:8-15.

of the troops. He says, "My father hath troubled the land." [5]
After the victory is won, the people seize the spoil to satisfy
their hunger and ignore the law prohibiting the eating of
flesh with the blood in it. Saul undertakes to remedy the
error but again is caught in the ambiguity of his roles.
To settle the issue, lots are cast and the blame falls upon
Jonathan who confesses his guilt in violating the order
against eating. He is saved from death by the intervention
of the people. Even more serious are the complications
which arise after the battle with the Amalekites. Saul's
conduct brings down upon him the judgment of the zealous
Samuel in the announcement that the kingdom is to be
taken away from him. In all these matters, the soul is
caught in the dilemma of diverse claims which it is unable
to reconcile in the presence of external demands that take
their toll of strength and put wisdom out of reach.

The inward drama moves on toward the end as David
appears upon the scene, first to neutralize the "evil spirit"
which possesses Saul, and then to engage more actively in
the affairs of the nation in preparation for his own accession to the throne. The effort to heal the breach in the soul
of Saul by music turns out to be only a palliative, and eventually David leaves the court to become leader of a movement operating independently of the crown. Henceforth,
these two stand apart in mutual contrast, one in decline,
the other in ascendancy.

---

[5] I Samuel 14:29.

As the conflict with the Philistines continues, David appears repeatedly with all the prowess that legend can supply. The victory in the Valley of Elah is a forecast of the future in which he is to be at the center of action. The mood of Saul changes quickly from the elation inspired by momentary triumph to jealous anger. Feeling the power of the kingship slipping from him, incensed by the praise given to David on account of his accomplishments, the energy needed to establish the position of Israel in security against enemies is dissipated in the satisfaction of personal passion. Saul "eyes" David "from that day on" and regards him continually as his enemy. He uses the enticement of marriage to his daughter, Michal, placing the price at one hundred foreskins of the Philistines, hoping thereby that David will fall at their hands. Frustrated in this attempt, he develops other means. He commands his son and his servants to act as his agents in killing David. Repeatedly, in a frenzied mood, his own hand is lifted in violence against his rival. When he hears that David is with Samuel at Ramah, he sends messengers in three relays to capture him, but, in each case, they are overwhelmed by the spirit of the dervishes and cannot take him. When Saul himself goes, he likewise is overcome and becomes so disoriented that he strips off his clothes and lies naked all night. Saul among the dervishes becomes current as a "proverb" in Israel.

At Gibeah, the King chides his officers about David, saying, "Will the son of Jesse give every one of you fields and vineyards, and make you all captains of thousands, and captains of hundreds?"[6] He derides them for conspiring against him and complains that no one has protected him against the league of his son and David. When, at his command, Ahimelech and his fellow priests who had served David at Nob are brought before him, he accuses them of giving sanctuary to David, and when Ahimelech praises David, Saul orders his servants to kill them. The officers decline to destroy the priests of the Lord, and Saul calls upon Doeg, captain of his herdsmen, an Edomite, to execute his command. Only Abiathar escapes to join David.[7] In this scene, the King acts out the internal disintegration which is soon to invite despair and defeat. His obsessive hostility toward David disperses his armies over the land and consumes strength which would have been better used to repel external attack. In the end, all efforts fail when David, paradoxically, negotiates successfully for temporary refuge in the territory of the Philistine enemy himself and Saul pursues him no more.

Saul's psychic extremity expressed in his visit to the witch of Endor is the prelude to the final acts of his career as Israel's first king.[8] The tradition which preserves these events shows the influence of prophetic thought and bias toward the party of Samuel, as it often does elsewhere. Even so, the tragic end on Mount Gilboa is a natural outcome of forces long at work in the soul of Saul. Death by his own hand is an act which expresses that ultimate frustration

[6] I Samuel 22:7,8.
[7] I Samuel 22:11-20.
[8] I Samuel 28:3-25.

which comes to a man when self is unable to integrate its native powers by responding to the call of nobler purpose than its own cause. Commanding physical stature, impressive outward appearance cannot withstand the onslaught of reality when internal forces rising from the primitive in man's nature—lawless impulse, jealous ambition, and passion—bring to naught the soul's quest for ordered fulfillment. Inward subversion unprotected by the armor of integrity, created by the action of God in the soul, ends in social failure.

2. *Renewing the Search for Unity and Integrity*

The kingship continues in David who, long before, in his relations with Saul, appears as a source of strength on guard against the destruction of the soul of Israel. His intimacy with Jonathan and his official duties in the house of Saul set forth clearly the constructive forces which are aligned on the side of the survival and further development of Israel's unique position in history. This is set forth dramatically in the Valley of Elah where the Philistines defy the armies of Saul. The legend of David's superiority in the contest with Goliath affirms that the soul of Israel cannot find security by exclusive reliance on the means which other nations employ in attaining their ambitions. The people may wish to have a king like their neighbors, but the sense of mission associated with Israel from the beginning must be preserved in every historical setting.

David's contribution to the maintenance of balance in

the soul is seen in his relations with Jonathan, on the one hand, and his restraint with respect to direct action against Saul, on the other. His friendship with the King's son is a meeting of minds and hearts, spontaneous and genuine, with a mutual loyalty that reveals a noble strength against the background of the unstable and jealous monarch. In the words, ". . . the soul of Jonathan was knit to the soul of David, and Jonathan loved him as his own soul," we have an impressive union of royalty by inheritance and royalty by unassuming integrity.[9] It is a relationship that makes it natural for Jonathan to invest David with his robe, his armor, and his sword, first as an expression of love, then as a symbol of his voluntary abdication of the throne in favor of his friend. When this confidence finds support in the deeds of David as a soldier and is confirmed by the approval of the people, it is clear that the resources in the soul of Israel are far from exhaustion.

David's attitude toward Saul is as circumspect as his love for Jonathan is sincere. When Saul, pursuing him, turns aside in the cave near Engedi where David and his men are hiding, David refrains from killing him, but cuts off a piece of his robe for the purpose of demonstrating later his loyalty to the king.[10] On another occasion when Saul is asleep in camp at night, his spear stuck in the ground near his head, David and Abishai take the spear and a jar of water which also belongs to Saul, but they do no violence to him.[11]

---

[9] I Samuel 18:1.

[10] I Samuel 24:4.

[11] I Samuel 26:6-12.

In these and other similar acts, David reveals devotion to a cause in which he is instrument and whose aims are to take precedence over his own wishes in major decisions. That this devotion is not uncorrupted by other motives is a fact of history. Nevertheless, the soul, conscious of its own power, seeks to use that power in such a way as to actualize events beyond present attainment and adds therefore to self-fulfillment. The inward strength to bring the past into relation with the present is manifest in David's classic lament over the fall of "the mighty" where he praises with unrivaled pathos the victories of Saul and the love of Jonathan which to him, was "wonderful, passing the love of women." [12]

But the transition to the new setting is not easily made. Anointed King of Judah at Hebron, David's first act is to send a message of gratitude to the men of Jabesh-gilead for their burial of Saul. Then he is confronted by Abner's plan to establish Saul's son, Ishbaal, as king of Israel beginning with the support of Gilead and Ephraim. The contest between David and the house of Saul, abetted by Joab on the one side and Abner on the other, eventually results in the union of north and south. Abner seeks alliance with David who receives his proposal with favor, but when Joab discovers the nature of Abner's visit, he charges that a plot is being formed. He sends messengers to bring Abner back and slays him ostensibly to avenge the death of his brother, Asahel, whom Abner had killed. These evils lurking in the

---

[12] II Samuel 1:17-26.

soul of Israel, waiting for more favorable occasion to overcome them, issue in a conspiracy which destroys Ishbaal as
he lies in his own bed. For this deed, David orders swift justice, and the elders of Israel go to Hebron where they anoint
him King over all Israel with the capital at Jerusalem.

The soul of Israel, at one with itself again in the integrity of David's devotion, recovers its hold on the earlier
commission given to Abraham in "Walk before me and be
thou perfect." The intervening years, in which successive
attempts are made to advance toward this goal, merge with
the present in a setting where the old faith must be reaffirmed and defended. The struggle goes on. The range of
emotion in the soul of David touches every chord of the
human heart. There is the triumph of military victory on
the frontiers. The Philistines are quiet on the western border. On the east, his conquests include Edom and Moab;
Syria as far as the Euphrates; and on the north to the foot
of the Lebanons. The Syrians become his servants and bring
gifts while King Tou, of Hamath, salutes David for reliev-
ing the pressure on his boundaries from Damascus. Such
accomplishments fill the soul with patriotic fervor, and put
into the heart of David the plan to build a house of the
Lord in Jerusalem. With a capital and the promise of unity
among the people, attachment to the land is strengthened.

So David reigned over all Israel; and David adminis-
tered justice and equity to all his people.[13]

---

[13] II Samuel 8:15. From the *Revised Standard Version of the Bible*,
copyrighted 1946 and 1952.

Among the leaders who serve David, none is more loyal and effective than Joab who rose in the King's favor as one of the "mighty men," along with his brothers, Abishai and Asahel, in the days when he was a fugitive from Saul. Bloody and brutal, enjoying the battle at times for its own sake, it must be said that Joab is basically faithful to David, though often in his impetuosity he is torn between what he thinks is good for his sovereign and what is good for himself. He is an able warrior, a skillful military leader. He knows the country well and plans the strategy for the battles it is necessary to fight. He knows how to deploy his men effectively against the enemy. A notable example of his ability is seen in the battle with the Ammonites who rebuff David's proffer of friendship and hire Hadadezer, of Syria, to fight with them. Joab meets them at Hamath, divides his forces with his brother, Abishai, in such a way as to separate the Ammonite forces from the Syrian, and undertakes a two-fold frontal attack. He leads the assault on the Syrians while Abishai faces the Ammonites. By this maneuver, the Syrians are thrown back and the Ammonites retire from the field. In the glory that he wins by astuteness in conducting his campaigns and by the ruthlessness with which he carries them out, he does not forget his King. When he has all but captured Rabbah, the royal city of the Ammonites, he sends for David that he may strike the final blow and receive the honors of the day. The message to the King read, ". . . encamp against the city, and take it; lest I take the city and it be called after my name." [14]

---

[14] II Samuel 12:28.

When Absalom organizes the revolt against David and
the issue comes to battle in the field, Joab ignores David's
plea to "deal gently with Absalom," and thrusts three darts
into his heart while he hangs by his head in a tree. Then,
when the victory is turned into mourning because the King
is overwhelmed with grief, Joab is incensed and rebukes
David, charging him with ingratitude to his people and to
his commanders who have saved the throne for him. He
commands him to appear in public and put away the
"shame" of showing sorrow for the enemy in his own house.
The conflicting emotions are described in the statement that
the people stole into the city as though they were fleeing
after defeat in battle instead of victory. It is Joab also who
disposes of Uriah, and after the defeat of Absalom dis-
patches his commander, Amasa. He protests David's proposal for taking a census of Israel but, in the end, carries
out the command and presents him with the figures cover-
ing the people from Dan to Beersheba. When the time
comes for the King to be gathered to his fathers, Joab supports Adonijah for his successor, but Nathan, the prophet,
and Bathsheba counteract his influence. In this phase of the
struggle of the soul of Israel to accommodate itself to the
rough situation of the time, Joab occupies the no-man's-
land of contending inner forces where issues are confused
and outcomes mingle evil with good intentions.

Of a different character, but partaking of some of the
qualities in Joab, is the position of Absalom, David's favorite son who is extolled in the words,

But in all Israel, there was none to be so much praised
as Absalom for his beauty: from the sole of his foot
even to the crown of his head there was no blemish in
him.[15]

Incited by the violation of his sister, Tamar, at the hands
of his half brother, Amnon, Absalom's intrigue to gain the
throne is temporarily halted by David. But, after a period
of hiding and enforced confinement, he coerces Joab to assist him in regaining his father's favor. With this new
liberty, he makes fresh plans. He acquires a chariot and
"fifty men to run before him." He rises early and stands by
the gate as the citizens come from various parts of the country for adjudication of their grievances before the King. He
makes friends with them. He inquires about the cities from
which they come and commends his capacity to render justice even better than his father. In this way, by persistent
effort to advance his cause, he "stole the hearts of the men
of Israel." The threat to David's power grows and the issue
is submitted ultimately to armed conflict. In the end, there
is defeat and death for Absalom and a broken heart for
David.

O my son Absalom, my son, my son Absalom! Would I
had died instead of you, O Absalom, my son, my son! [16]

Nearer to the center of the soul in David's time is the
prophet, Nathan, who, in contrast with other figures who
dominate the scene around the King, represents the rare

---

[15] II Samuel 14:25.
[16] II Samuel 18:33. (RSV)

appearance of articulate conscience. It is he who perceives the acts of David in their true light and, though winking at or allowing many of them to pass, chooses one occasion to bring him to judgment in no uncertain terms. The charge is so stated that the King's own sense of right and wrong pronounces the sentence. In the parable of the rich man who had many sheep in his flocks, but who, on the occasion of a visit by a guest, takes the one sheep that a poor man has, Nathan draws the inescapable parallel with Uriah whose death was deliberately planned by David in order to make Bathsheba available. The verdict, "Thou art the man," falls like a millstone upon the ears of the King. Though this sin may be forgiven, the soul cannot empty itself of what has become its content by premeditated act. Inward decision cannot be revoked. Therefore, "The sword shall not depart from thy house," and this thing will be done, not secretly, but before all Israel.[17] Nevertheless, the wife he has stolen is chosen to be the mother of the son who will sit upon the throne after him and build the house of the Lord which it is not given him to build. The soul is caught in the toils of acute moral conflict. It falls short of the inward mastery needed really to unite the nation. Hope lives on in the possibility of reinstating the power of the old faith in a new situation. The intention to build a house of the Lord is an expression of the soul's effort to regain grip on its past as it moves toward the future. But, as we shall see, danger lurks in this also.

17 II Samuel 12:7-12.

The contest for the throne following the death of David takes the pattern of the days immediately after the fall of Saul at Gilboa. With Amnon and Absalom out of the running, Adonijah seems to Joab and Abiathar the logical candidate and Adonijah himself is not reticent about pressing his claim. His father has never "displeased him" by questioning any of his acts as he had not in the case of Absalom, but others in important positions at David's court have plans of their own, and they have the ear of the King. Before Adonijah can organize the necessary support from his followers, David acts to have Solomon formally anointed. With his hopes thus ended, Adonijah seeks the protection of the altar and, on appeal to Solomon, receives a temporary reprieve for his precipitate move to take the throne. Later he makes the mistake of requesting, through Bathsheba, that Abishag be given him for a wife. Solomon, aware that Adonijah still has influential support in Israel, seizes upon this request as a pretext to have him put to death by the hand of Benaiah. In due course, Abiathar and Joab also are eliminated, the priest confined to his house at Anathoth, and the warrior killed before the altar. In like manner, others whose deeds in their relation to David warranted it are cut down.

So the kingdom was established in the hand of Solomon.[18]

---

[18] I Kings 2:46.

3. *Decay in the Cloak of Splendor*

In the reign of Solomon, the soul of Israel continues the struggle for mastery over the forces which had taken hold of David and the people in the consolidation of the monarchy and in the extension of the boundaries of power to far-flung frontiers. The focus, however, is now in the single enterprise which Solomon inherits from his father and is destined to complete—the building of the house of the Lord. The new king loses no time in proceeding with this undertaking which is drawn to proportions and invested with a splendor that comes, in time, to make his name the synonym of wisdom and regal power. The international situation is exceedingly favorable, offering release from the constant external threats that had drawn off the energy of the people from earliest times. Moreover, there is a promising degree of internal unity. The prosperity of David's time continues. In his early overtures with Hiram, King of Tyre, who had been under obligation to David for military protection and food supplies, Solomon refers to his father's preoccupation with wars that diverted him from his purpose to build, and adds that he has "rest on every side" and there is "neither adversary nor misfortune." As for the people,

> Judah and Israel were many, as the sand which is by the sea in multitude, eating and drinking and making merry.[19]

---

[19] I Kings 4:20.

At the beginning of his reign, Solomon's attitude is marked by a humility that reflects his view of the greatness of his task. He feels like a child, not knowing "how to go out or come in," and he prays for an understanding heart to govern his people. But prayer cannot avoid seeking answer by utilizing external means for the realization of internal purpose. Government has already attained significant proportions requiring a kind of bureaucracy which could establish official links with all the regions that are subject to Jerusalem. These powers must be extended to accomplish the work in hand. The wisdom of Solomon, made legendary by certain dramatic episodes, is primarily a matter of political sagacity and administrative genius. His marriage with the daughter of Pharaoh, king of Egypt, is the first step toward strengthening his relations with foreign powers, and this is followed later by similar alliances with the Moabites, Ammonites, Edomites, Sidonians, and Hittites. Administratively he has, in addition to the normal personnel of the court, twelve officers over as many sections of the country. These are responsible for supplying him with all needed provisions. Taxes from the households and tribute from the kingdoms bordering the Euphrates, Philistia, and Egypt must be collected to finance the enterprise now under way. Moreover, the requisite materials and special skills not available in Israel must be secured outside the kingdom. Hiram becomes the main source of these.

Finally, for the cutting of the timber in the forests of Lebanon, for its transportation from the sea to the top of Mount Zion, for the quarrying and shaping of stones and

metals, enormous quantities of manpower are needed.
Forced labor, which was introduced in the time of David,
is now taken for granted. Thirty thousand men are sent to
the forests in relays of ten thousand per month to cut the
cedar that must be brought. In addition, there are seventy
thousand burden bearers and eighty thousand stonecutters
and masons, requiring thirty-three hundred overseers. As
the King commanded,

> They brought great stones, costly stones, and hewed
> stones, to lay the foundation of the house. And Solo-
> mon's builders and Hiram's builders did hew them,
> and the stone squarers: so they prepared timber and
> stones to build the house.[20]

The time required for the completion of the temple was
seven years; for the King's palace, thirteen years. The ceremonies of dedication, including Solomon's address and the
assignment of the priests to their duties with a completed
building that was a noble work of many hands, consum-
mated the hope of Israel that the God of their fathers, no
longer a wanderer with his people, would now enjoy their
own permanently settled condition.

The house of the Lord recapitulates the aspirations nurtured by solitary altars in the towns and countrysides close
to the daily life of the people, the portable tent of meeting
of the wilderness, and seeks to enshrine in splendid abode
the spirit of the Eternal forever. It is the beginning of a

---

20 I Kings 5:17,18.

new stage in the religion of Israel whereby the soul is contained in ceremony, ritual, and vicarious act with increasing separation from everyday engagement with the common life. Along with this, and perhaps an expression of the growing hospitality to the culture of the lands of the East, is the increase in the altars of alien gods, even the incorporation of their symbols in the temple itself, whereas it was hinted when the building began that a shrine so nobly conceived and furnished would, by its very magnificence, deal a final blow to these deities.

The opposite turns out to be the case. Solomon's love of foreign women softens his heart toward their gods and opens the way for extending their worship. The abominations of human sacrifice to Chemosh and Molech appear. Such is the amplitude of tolerance in a time when wealth and pride contribute to the blurring of distinctions and the discipline of single-mindedness is absent. Thus at the very moment when the resources of the nation are mobilized and extended in the formal exaltation of its God, a deterioration in integrity is taking place. This ambiguity in the soul of Israel becomes the incentive for the rise of external counteracting forces, some of them evil in themselves, but calculated to serve as a discipline that will restore the balance of a central and controlling purpose. On the horizons of the kingdom, neighbors who suffer from old injuries and chafe under current burdens of tribute begin to assert themselves. Hadad, a survivor from Joab's brutal raid on Edom, nurtured by Pharaoh of Egypt, comes seeking revenge.

Rezon, of Syria, likewise "was an adversary of Israel all the days of Solomon, doing mischief as Hadad did." [21] Beyond these are greater threats biding their time.

But external aggression is not all that clouds the clear skies which had looked down with such favor upon Solomon. Jeroboam, the son of Nebat, able official of the King, director of the forced labor in the north, is stirred by the prophet Ahijah who suggests by a symbolic oracle that he is to be an instrument of the Lord in the crisis ahead. When Solomon hears this, he plans to destroy Jeroboam who, to avert the threat, takes refuge in Egypt where he remains under the protection of King Shishak until Solomon's death. Then when Rehoboam, the natural heir to the throne, goes to Shechem to be installed as king, Jeroboam appears as the spokesman of "all the assembly of Israel," saying:

> Your father made our yoke heavy. Now therefore lighten the hard service of your father and his heavy yoke upon us, and we will serve you.[22]

These are momentous words touching a vital need in the soul of Israel that is destined to become a central issue in the changing scenes of the future.

Rehoboam forsakes the wiser counsel of the elders who had served his father and follows the harsher advice of the young men who had grown up with him. His answer to Jeroboam and all Israel is this:

---

[21] I Kings 11:25. (RSV)
[22] I Kings 12:4. (RSV)

My father made your yoke heavy, but I will add to your yoke; my father chastised you with whips, but I will chastise you with scorpions.[23]

The people answer,

What portion have we in David? We have no inheritance in the son of Jesse. To your tents, O Israel.[24]

From this time forth, the kingdom stands divided with the name that formerly designated the people as a whole taken over by the north to distinguish it from Judah in the south. Rehoboam continues to reign at Jerusalem while Jeroboam occupies the seat as ruler of the north in Shechem. One of the first acts of Jeroboam is to set up shrines in his own territory so that the people will no longer need to go to Jerusalem and perchance be drawn away from their allegiance to him. He makes priests for the alien altars, consecrating any who wish to serve. Warnings are given by prophets in the midst, but he ignores them. His successors in the north, and Rehoboam's in the south, alternate between periods of stability and periods of disintegration. Periodically the two groups go to war against each other while encroachments of outside powers begin to reduce the two kingdoms to a state of helplessness and ultimately to servility. The house of God is emptied of an increasing number of its worshipers who are now despoiled by division and idolatry. Ordeal to recapture the old simplicity, laid deeply in a subconscious past and ruled by conscience, is

---

[23] I Kings 12:14. (RSV)
[24] I Kings 12:16. (RSV)

now at issue in the challenge to reason's exalted splendor.

Looking back on these events, who will fail to see in Israel's travail the tides and crosscurrents of the peculiar dynamics common to human beings everywhere? The wavering of Saul, his intention to do right but by ineptitude and vagrant impulse yielding to wrong; his dissipation of precious power in vain pursuit of an able fellow countryman whom he saw through delusion; his final degradation and the discomfiture of his people before the enemy—are not all these outcomes of tendencies to be found in the unconscious of all men? The heroic stature of David won by skill and courage and capacity to bind others to him in undying loyalty; his gift for deep mutuality in friendship, his noble thought of building a sanctuary to keep the holy unsullied from unclean hands; all these countered by weakness in use of power for crime against the innocent, by failure as a father, opening the way for intrigue in his own house, with vengeance and reprisal all around him—are not such traits the signs of inward forces battling for some resolution through alliance with a power beyond self? The regal Solomon resplendent in his dominion at home and abroad, the mixed motives of loyalty to the past and his hospitality to foreign deities; his exploitation of the people by exacting labor and taxes; his quelling of revolt while old enemies prepare to resume their assault; the truculence of his successor in closing the doors of justice and democracy —are not these the symptoms of sin in high places at all times and among all peoples? Are not these the marks of a human predicament which constantly calls for salvation?

If so, whence shall it come and how shall it be appropriated? For answer we shall look first to the arbiters of crisis in Israel.

4. *Prophylaxis for Crisis*

In the face of the political and moral deterioration of the middle years, two sets of forces, complementary in their effects, are at work to keep the balance in the soul of Israel. The great powers to the east, recuperating from their state of decline, return to the attack looking with envious eyes upon the prosperity of the land and the treasure left by Solomon at Jerusalem. Among these, Assyria is the first to advance into Israel, beginning with threats that end in temporary settlements for tribute and gradually leading to the siege and destruction of Samaria in the time of Hoshea. Judah in the south continues until the rise of Nebuchadnezzar who destroys Jerusalem and carries away both people and treasure to Babylon. The final blow crushes the national sovereignty, already divided, and leaves Jerusalem in ruins.

But the end is not yet. From the call of Abraham until the day his descendants marched back captive beyond the Euphrates, there had been in the soul of Israel a sense of destiny undergirded by a faith in the future that survived all changes and compromises. Under the pressure of political and economic necessity, incident to settlement in the land and the consolidation of the tribes into a nation, this inner purpose often yielded to the exigencies of the hour and jeopardized integrity. But, just as a man stricken with a disease that threatens his life marshals all his reserves to meet the crisis, so Israel, in the day of deterioration and devastation, brought forth agents of salvation. It is in the years following the fall of Jerusalem that we see the clearest result of this spirit, but long before that time there was preparation for the final crisis in the accumulative and intensified reassertion of moral insights that could be tapped when the emergency came. This was chiefly the work of Moses and the prophets.

The prophets do not appear in full stature all at once. They have a history. The beginnings we see in tracing their function seem no different from the seers, sorcerers, diviners, among other ancient peoples. They are presumed to be in touch with the supernatural. They have special powers for seeing what is hidden from ordinary eyes and for performing acts that express their command over powers not available to average men. Thus Saul can consult Samuel for direction in finding his father's asses. The stories of Elisha are suffused with the extraordinary and miraculous. But in Israel, as among no other people of ancient times, there is a development that transcends all these early beginnings. The prophet acquires a special role in relation to events. He anticipates and shapes history. He is, therefore, associated with important leaders and rulers. He is consulted in advance of important undertakings such as the declaration of war, or preparations for battle, or for the building of a sacred dwelling. He is one who stands apart from the people and develops powers of acute observation which are not common to those who are deeply involved in the affairs of everyday life. He is the instrument of a Power above himself, and to whom he feels subject, though he is not dissociated from the fortunes of his people. Indeed, it is his vocation to serve the interests of his people in ways which oftentimes are not acceptable to them because what he says is in criticism of their views and ambitions. He is the spokesman for the primacy of the internal life, and his counsel is frequently rejected in Israel on account of the urgency of external demands.

But it is significant that when Israel progressively declines as a political power, the prophets become more active and begin to demonstrate a capacity for judgment they have not shown before. When the kings fail, the great hour of the prophet comes. One of the most vigorous and picturesque of these is Elijah. His relations with Ahab of Israel are filled with drama. Human nature in this setting is at its worst, and the man who is called to warn the king does his work in relays alternating between periods of deep fear and depression and moments of high courage and vigorous denunciation. The earlier prophets like Nathan and Elijah delivered their messages in the form of parables and oracles. The later prophets, whose outlook inspired the Second Law, Deuteronomy, and who did so much to shape the religion of Israel in its final form, adopted writing as their mode of communication. Insurgent and radical in spirit, they express that inner vitality which returns to power when external confusion threatens the soul's mastery of events. They seek emancipation from outmoded institutional practices and a renewal of purpose that opens the way toward ethical maturity in a setting of ampler opportunity. The deposit of their influence and its implications for our understanding of the adventure of personality will be our concern in the next chapter.

3. THE LATTER YEARS

UTTERLY DESOLATE AFTER THE DESTRUCTION of Jerusalem in 586 B.C. and the carrying away into Babylon, the soul of Israel enters a new era of confusion, reorientation, and decision. The age of the monarchy under Saul, David, and Solomon, marked by successive triumphs that issued in a supreme position among the nations, ends in disaster. The temple which was to guarantee the perpetual exaltation of the spirit of Israel is now violated by the pillage and greed of secular powers. The final blow does not come without warning. More than a century before Nebuchadnezzar lays siege to Jerusalem, Samaria is overrun by Assyria and left without strength to rise again. Now it is all over for Judah, too. The last bastions of Mount Zion are shattered.

What is left for the soul to do when the material and political structures upon which it has relied for security and permanence go to pieces? First, it seeks to come to terms with immediate demands, to make the best of a bad situation, until it can again get its bearings. The will to live remains even though the conditions that formerly made that life satisfactory no longer exist. The external enemy must be met on such terms as one can get. Submission to forces alien to the soul of Israel is not a new experience and, for the moment, a re-enactment of the distress of other days can be endured, although the dimensions are changed and the humiliation overwhelming. The shock must be absorbed, the pieces put together in some sort of pattern while one waits in hope for more favorable events. There is some satisfaction, of course, in the thought that one does not surrender without resistance, that life holds on to its ruins in the conviction that another house will rise upon them. Fortunes have been known to shift in the past and that offers the suggestion that they may change again for the better.

But all this is temporary. An ordinary people can bring itself to accept the outcomes of battle, admitting that to the strongest battalions belong the victory, while hoping that its strength can be rebuilt to the point of challenging the victor and reversing defeat. This is in the minds of the leaders of Israel. But there is a more searching question. Instead of explaining their unhappy state by simple reference to the power of the eastern kings, before whom the armies of Israel were all but powerless, there are those who dare to ask the question, Why did this happen to us? What conditions in our life are responsible for this event? Those who take this inward look stand over against those who look to the external facts of the inadequacy of Israel's arms and the superiority of the enemy in the field and before the walls. Though there are obvious causes of misfortune outside ourselves, it is equally obvious that the power of another over us points to a deficit in our own resources. It is in the balancing of these two factors in human existence that we discover the strength of the soul of Israel. This strength has its source in the fact that the issues of life are not discerned by a literal reading of results apparent in the relative positions of physical forces. They are to be found in the inward judgment of right and wrong collaborating with meanings which transcend all particular occasions. This is the outstanding insight in the history which we are examining.

Consequently, beneath all the superficial answers to questions about Israel's plight, there lies the deeper, constantly recurring, issue related to essential character and mission. Being true to oneself, in the fullest stature of human possibility, continues to be one of the basic premises of the reasoning in the latter years. As we have seen already, this is not worked out formally but dynamically, not as systematized treatise but as living engagement with history. We are to view it now in the final scenes of political humiliation and threatened inward dissolution.

1. Crisis and the Growth of Self-Consciousness

It is the function of crisis to throw people back upon themselves. When all supports in material and institutional arrangements are taken away, it is then that an individual or a nation asks, Who am I? or Who are we? What criteria remain to give substance to self-affirmation? Again and again in the Old Testament, these questions appear, clothed in the vitality of inescapable concreteness, and never more acutely than when Sargon takes Samaria and Nebuchadnezzar leads the captives away from Jerusalem. It is under the challenge of two crises that the soul of Israel evolves— two historic events, one of which culminates in a memorable deliverance endowed with mighty acts and inspiring sentiments, and the other whose outcome is despair in the subversion of national existence. Between the one and the other, the answer to "Who am I?" is worked out into a final mode of self-consciousness.

When we speak of being thrown back upon oneself, we mean, mainly, that one re-examines his past, makes inventory of all that the soul contains, and appraises resources which may be gathered to meet the crisis through a reorientation of meaning and purpose. This is the process which we see in Israel and to which the prophets make their great contribution. It begins to be articulate in Amos, first of the writing prophets, and continues in the activity of his successors Hosea, Isaiah, Micah, Jeremiah, Ezekiel, and others. All these are great individuals, men of acute moral and religious insight, who stand apart from their predecessors in the "schools of the prophets," and receive their messages out of their brooding on the events of their times in relation to the fate of their people.

In all these prophets, the soul of Israel undergoes severe self-scrutiny to determine on what grounds integrity may now be maintained. The search begins with Amos who sees not only the devastation in prospect from outside sources,

but the disintegration that already exists as a result of the
division between official Israel and the masses of the common folk. He sees with keen eye the gathering storm on the
far horizons destined to sweep down upon his people. That,
however, is background. In the foreground is the threat of
imbalance in the soul, the conflict between the needs of the
masses and the power and pride of the wealthy, the violence
in the exploitation of the one by the other. The outward
menace is enough to strike terror in the heart, but the internal condition to whose character the former testifies is
even worse, for it is destroying the soul itself. The message
of Amos is drawn to the pattern of the consequences which
he sees. It is not overstated, for external disaster can be endured if the soul remains intact. If it does not, all is lost.

Amos pronounces judgment on two evils—injustice in the
practices of official Israel toward the poor, and the sanctifi-
cation of these practices by the religious institutions. Taken
together, the main charge is the violation of the solidarity
of rulers and people through an unequal appropriation of
the blessings of the land to which is added the extrava-
gances of luxurious complacency. The poor are trampled in
the dust; the weak are crushed; honest men are despoiled
by bribes; law is subverted to evil purposes by the strong;
robbery and violence fill the houses of the rich; the sins of
ingratitude and hypocrisy corrupt human relations. For
these unnumbered crimes, retribution will be quick and
thorough for the very reason that special favor has been
shown to Israel in the deliverance from Egypt, and the purpose of that is now compromised. Faithlessness and unright-

eousness call for appropriate punishment. As surely as there is a connection between events in nature, there is a connection in the internal life between what is right and what is wrong, and each produces its consequences. Despite all warnings, evil conduct goes on, even in the very presence of the altars of religion. Sin is ritualized. Swift and sure judgment is at hand. The unworthy kingdom will be wiped out.

> The virgin of Israel is fallen; she shall no more rise: she is forsaken upon her land; there is none to raise her up.[1]

For sheer majesty of conscience, in plea for righteousness under impending doom, and stark contempt for the thin veneer of religious pretension, bred by prosperity, the message of Amos is an unrivaled classic, a flaming epitaph for the reign of Jeroboam II.

Hosea, a contemporary of Amos, takes up the same theme of judgment, but his message is tempered by another emphasis which he presents in dramatic oracle. Under the figure of the wife, taken in harlotry, who has borne him children having names that describe the rejection of Israel, he advances to the view that the divine love manifested toward the nation cannot go permanently without result. When judgment has purged the soul of its iniquity, an unfailing love will provide redemptive healing and restoration.

In similar tone, Isaiah begins his message directed to Judah as Amos had spoken his to North Israel. At his con-

---

[1] Amos 5:2.

secration in the temple he confesses that he is a "man of unclean lips . . . living among a people of unclean lips." [2] The soul of Israel, inwardly corrupt, cannot obtain favor by burnt offerings, by the "fat of fed beasts," by festivals, no matter how precise the ritual or how correct the ceremony may be. Though the coming judgment is inescapable, yet by his own inward purification, by a personally redemptive insight, Isaiah is able to offer hope for the future, whereas Amos had limited his message to a settled verdict from which appeal is impossible. The hope which the prophet sees, however, rests upon the maintenance of integrity in Israel's purpose and refusal to effect alliances whose outcomes are doomed to fail before a child is old enough to call his parents by name.[3] In all his counsels to the kings of Judah during his time, the prophet holds tenaciously to the view that only steadfast loyalty to the basic genius of Israel can bring the people through all their trials to ultimate victory. His words, "In returning and rest you shall be saved; in quietness and in trust shall be your strength" are the keynote of all he says in the varying situations that he faces.[4] In the soul of Isaiah we see that inner certitude which before all the odds of desperate alternatives makes a man a "hiding-place from the wind . . . , the shade of a great rock in a weary land." [5] Though his counsel is not heeded, because confusion and hysteria possess the people,

---

[2] Isaiah 6:5. (Moffatt)

[3] Isaiah 8:4.

[4] Isaiah 30:15. (RSV)

[5] Isaiah 32:2. (RSV)

his word survives as a monument to high purpose, while his faith in a loyal remnant is the grain of mustard seed enfolding the future hope.

Micah likewise insists that above all else, integrity is the essential quality of the soul. In language that reveals that he, like Amos, is advocate for the people of the towns and countrysides, he foresees punishment for those who plan wickedness on their beds at night and in the morning seize the houses and fields of the poor and rob them of their inheritance. If the question is asked, How may the coming perils be averted? the answer is not in terms of more offerings and sacrifices, but in ethical living, in doing justly, in loving mercy, in walking "humbly with thy God." [6]

Among all the great prophets, none appears in more pathetic setting, or in greater heroic stature, than Jeremiah. In him the soul of Israel surges with all the crosscurrents and tides of frenzied patriotism, faced by overwhelming odds, and the sanity of aspirations molded to the high destiny in which he held faith until the end. Called to undertake an impossible task, timid to the point of self-evacuation, harassed by fears that are not imaginary, he girds himself with confidence in the truth that possesses him and, by an unassailable faith, stands his ground while the earth gives way under his feet. In all the charges which he brings against his people, none goes closer to the mark than the question in his great temple sermon,

Is it not themselves, to their own confusion? [7]

6 Micah 6:8.
7 Jeremiah 7:19. (RSV)

In the last analysis the crucial issue does not reside in what others do, threatening though that may be, but in inward decision that accords with right. In the capacity to organize chaos into a life that will survive all ruin, in that lies the dignity of man. It is the living monument built out of the battle to save the soul of his people, while struggling with his own soul, that posterity accords Jeremiah the accolade. This, too, is human nature, made again under God.

In Ezekiel we see the most extreme reaction of all the prophets to the Babylonian captivity. As a participant in it, he feels its full impact. In the oracles delivered at Jerusalem during the early period of his ministry, he is merciless in his declaration of judgment upon the nation. Not only will the sword, famine, and pestilence destroy the people, but the few who survive will be made to serve the purpose of advertising the hated abominations which Israel has adopted from her neighbors. In two oracles containing the most vivid, if not vile, sexual imagery, he draws a picture of human nature that scarcely stops short of total depravity. In Ezekiel the soul of Israel turns upon itself the vehemence and fury aroused by the brutality so thoroughly executed by external enemies. That so many of the customs of these foreigners have been appropriated by the people, that so many love what should be hated, is cause for the utmost of fanatical revulsion.

The measure of this reaction is manifest in the prophet's swift and extensive flights into fantasy. An unleashed imagination enables him to annihilate space and overrun all barriers to movement from desperation to ecstasy. In the twinkling of an eye, he mounts on wings and visits places unknown in heaven or earth. As his body sinks in the quicksands of engulfing reality, he lays hold of the air and lifts himself by the bootstraps of his own unfettered zeal. Nearly every vestige of the older order is renounced, especially the institution of religion whose corruption is the cause of the destruction that has come. A new temple, purged from sanctified evils, rises on foundations not made with hands ready to be equipped with means to make it proof against defilement forever. There is to be no temporizing, no countenancing of any existing good upon which a better order might be built. No! Only a complete housecleaning will suffice. Reformation must be as thorough and as devastating as the enemy has been in his conquest, for that is the measure of the internal decay.

In two instances, however, Ezekiel comes down to earth. One appears in his work as pastor among the exiles. In this he confronts the reality of their condition in need of consolation, and deals with the problem of the individual in a cruel world. This ministry, however, is not much more than the comfort that one finds in the thought that eventually, when the tables are turned, the misery one now endures will be visited on those who have caused it. The note of retribution is very strong in Ezekiel. The other instance in which he seeks to come to terms with reality appears in the latter chapters of the Book where, committed to a program of holiness, he recognizes that religion cannot be trusted to the masses and that adequate safeguards must be prepared against future corruption. Therefore, for the new temple which he envisions, there must be a corresponding ritual to protect its purity from the intrusion of outside influences. In this, the prophet Ezekiel surrenders to his priestly intuitions. Aside from the encouragement which his visions brought to a depressed people, this latter emphasis is probably the prophet's main contribution to his time.

The mood of the Second Isaiah, while retaining the emphasis upon the necessity of judgment on the moral history of Israel, presents a marked contrast to that which pervades Ezekiel. This prophet has a similar gift for flights of imagination, but it is characterized by the buoyancy and confidence which he feels in the presence of a change in the historical situation that offers favorable prospect for the return of the exiles. His message (Isaiah 40-55) is a hymn announcing, in rhythmic cadence, the coming deliverance and restoration. His opening words are in the high key of an optimism that affirms the end of wars of expiation, the full payment of penalty, and the boon of forgiveness. But this end is also a beginning, a renewal of the soul of Israel that fulfills the best in its past and leads to accomplishment beyond all former expectations. The core of the latter is contained in a series of oracles about the Lord's servant variously related to the prophet himself and to the future nation as a whole. In so far as the inner logic of his utterances can be discerned, it appears that in Israel's own experience of being judged and punished, the nation has earned the right and privilege of witnessing to the meaning of righteousness and justice before all the earth. The extraordinary manner in which this has been accomplished by a succession of tragedies, apostasies, and recoveries, the holy people of the Lord are about to receive their vindication and their exaltation in ennobled service.

> Behold my servant, whom I uphold, my chosen, in whom my soul delights; I have put my spirit upon him, he will bring forth justice to the nations.[8]

This new order in human relations is emphasized by the prophet's rhapsodic references to the beauty and fertility with which even nature is to be endowed. His words are the overflow of a sensitive mind exuberant with the joy of a valiant faith issuing in a strengthened conviction with respect to the future. Most important of all is the declaration that coming events will establish forever the sovereignty of the God whose providence and power through all vicissitudes have remained intact, and who, by the ultimate victory of his people, will be entitled to universal reign.

> Break forth together into singing, you waste places of Jerusalem; for the Lord has comforted his people, he has redeemed Jerusalem. The Lord has bared his holy arm before the eyes of all the nations; and all the ends of the earth shall see the salvation of our God.[9]

The latter years, as we are thinking of them, came to their close with the establishment of a religious community as a result of the edict of Cyrus whose accession to power over Babylonia inspired the Second Isaiah and whose successors supported the work of Ezra and Nehemiah. But

---

[8] Isaiah 42:1. (RSV)
[9] Isaiah 52:9,10. (RSV)

preparation for this had been made three quarters of a century earlier in the reign of Josiah of Judah through the appearance of an extraordinary document known as the Second Law or Deuteronomy. The authors of this book, probably priestly in their outlook, were imbued by the ethical and religious insights of the prophets, and sought to reshape the law of the covenant in the spirit of their messages. The evidence seems to warrant the view that the Deuteronomists, in producing this version of the law, were attempting to solve the practical problem of perpetuating the high prophetic teaching in a form that could be appropriated and practiced by the common people.[10] The work ascribed to Moses, whose prestige and authority as the author of the original covenant were accepted, attributes to him the qualities of "prophet" also. It recapitulates the history of the exodus to the giving of the commandments at Sinai, restates and reinterprets these events in the light of later developments, and emphasizes by reiteration and elaboration the relation between Israel and her God.

> For you are a people holy to the Lord your God; the Lord your God has chosen you to be a people for his own possession, out of all the peoples that are on the face of the earth. It was not because you were more in number than any other people . . . for you were the fewest of all peoples; but it is because the Lord loves you, and is keeping the oath which he swore to your fathers. . . .[11]

---

[10] Pfeiffer, R. H., *Introduction to the Old Testament*, p. 180. New York: Harper & Brothers, 1941.

[11] Deuteronomy 7:6-8. (RSV)

The meaning of this covenant is made clear with painstaking care, the central fact being that if the people of
Israel obey this law scrupulously, they will enjoy the blessings of the most favored land to which they are going. If
the Passover, the Sabbath, the appointed feasts, the ritual
requirements and obligations toward neighbor and so-
journer are observed, then the Lord God, with unfailing
love, will fulfill all his promises making his people favored
and fruitful above all others. If on the other hand they are
negligent and faithless the sufferings of the past will be re-
visited upon them. They will "serve . . . enemies whom the
Lord will send against" them "in hunger and thirst, in
nakedness, and in want of all things; and he will put a yoke
of iron upon" their "neck until he has destroyed" them.[12]
This law, supplemented by the code of holiness (Leviticus
17-26) and reaffirmed by Ezra, becomes the basis of the future Jewish community.

A much more elaborate statement than we have given
would be required to do full justice to all that the Old
Testament contains, not to mention the developments of
the Hellenistic period that follow the conquests of Alexander the Great and ultimately end in the coming of the
Romans in 63 B.C. Some of these omissions will find a place
in another context of our study as they may contribute to
the purpose we have in hand. For the present we must again
take a look backward in order to be better prepared for our
further journey. We must formulate, in summary, the

---

[12] Deuteronomy 28:48. (RSV)

meaning of our data in relation to the two interests expressed in the title of this book—the nature of human nature and the meaning of God in human experience.

2. *Human Nature in Engagement with Nature*

In this account of the developing soul of Israel, sketching a
succession of situations extending over a period of nearly
two thousand years, what have we learned about human
nature that has continuing validity? We know, of course,
that we are looking at the Old Testament record through
the eyes of men who were motivated by purposes which they
thought important, and that the materials were shaped and
reshaped in no small degree to these ends. But that in itself
is human nature, the same human nature that we have in
ourselves and that is working at this moment in these pages.
What we must keep in mind is that in serving the very aims
they felt important, they lived in and used actual situations
for their understanding of the meaning of life, and left to
us not only their views about events but descriptions of the
events themselves, chief among which are the internal
events, the deposit of time in the soul. When we study the
Bible, therefore, we are looking at the soul behaving, learning what it is by observing what it does, discovering, if we
can, its characteristic ways; and we are doing this in a time
perspective that enhances validity in an extraordinary manner. We are able to see things together in a wholeness that
reveals the nature of the parts and contributes meanings
which overflow the boundaries of particular times and lim-

ited occasions. What then do we observe to be characteristic of human nature in the Old Testament? In what ways is Hebrew man like all men and in what ways is he unique?

First of all, we see that human nature, here as elsewhere, has the animal need to persist, to survive. Physical hunger drives in the direction of securing from environment that which sustains the body. In the wild state, this means predation, living at the cost of death to other animals, or, if herbivorous, living out of the plentiful harvest of the plant kingdom or, perchance, living off both other animals and plants. The simplest form of adaptation for survival is direct consumption of what in the state of nature is ready to be eaten and assimilated. Among the lower animals, this demands equipment of the right kind of teeth, methods of attack, strength and skill, and a habitat that makes a living readily available. Adaptation at the most primitive level is an organ response to the conditions and provisions of environment.

It is true that man shares with the animals this need to use physical environment for purposes of survival, but when we first meet him, even in his most primitive state, he is much more than animal. He is not passive to the world as it presents itself; he has initiative for modifying environment, for shaping means to ends—a stick or stone or both tied together to make a weapon. He is an animal with human ways which means basically that he can take his environment, literally, in hand. He acts on it as well as in it, and is able to improve his techniques in ever-widening range.

Even when we meet him as solitary hunter, he exhibits this trait in elemental form.

Abraham, therefore, appears in history as a very highly developed human being. Centuries of progress in adaptation lay behind him. For one thing, certain animals had been completely domesticated, adapted to human purposes, supplying products for food, clothing, and shelter, and all portable on foot for continuous availability. Some of these animals had been put into service to carry the human body and its baggage. Other advances were commonplace. A lump of clay taken from the banks of an oasis or brook could be shaped into a drinking vessel, used to convey water from one place to another, or dropped into a well to be drawn up by a rope of skins. A skin itself could be made into a container. All these and more were available equipment for Abraham when he, with flocks and families, journeyed from Haran into Canaan. Living in this way is human nature; that is, the adaptation of physical nature to human purposes.

A second characteristic trait of human nature, as intimated in the preceding paragraph, is to have an occupation. The word itself is interesting. As we think of it, it means that with which one occupies himself with a special reference to time. That, however, was not its original significance. Actually, in terms of human development, the word refers to the act of occupying, to finding and filling space, location in environment. In Abraham's day, people were not so tense about time as they are today. Not the measure of work alone, but a place to settle was the important matter. On it depended resources for self-maintenance, comfort, and fruitfulness, which simply took the courses of the seasons in man and beast. Occupation is man's adaptation of himself, a relating of his powers to manage environment for the sake of ends in view, a refinement of his manipulative skill.

Occupying space, however, presents more than the problem of mobility, of movement to the most favorable place, or settlement in habitat and holding the ground. Moving in with all that one has requires caution. For a time, one can expect some courtesy and hospitality as a guest, but if one requires much space, the local residents will feel crowded. Technique for getting along with people must be developed. If one gets into trouble over a well in a place where water is scarce, one had better move on, or find a way to extend his welcome. By trial and error, one learns the economy of understandings and agreements as the basis of more permanent order in relationships. Mutual acknowledgment of competitive interests, mutual respect, and kindness are also human nature, and they go a long way in resolving the conflicts which arise in simple face-to-face relationships. The other side of competition, of course, is the fact that a man needs his neighbor as a market for his goods, so he is not only a man to be feared, but a man to be cultivated. Balance is kept by seeing the two sides of competition in perspective.

But economic self-maintenance, including the art of making oneself acceptable to one's neighbors, is not all that goes to make up human living. There are inherited customs, ways of thinking and feeling about oneself, values which justify the effort that goes into daily work. Most of all, there is one's family, wives and sons, in the midst of whom one has his being, and through whom he perpetuates himself. There is the feeling of solidarity in sharing the meanings handed down in traditions concerning the race to which one belongs, the strengthening of human ties by enduring hardship together, by co-operative achievement, by the joys of fertility, by increasing mastery over nature and oneself, by growing confidence in the future as one watches his sons founding families and rising to positions of leadership in the clans. There are also questions and doubts about all these things.

Outside this circle of immediate intimacy, in the larger environment, there are the wonders of the earth with its towering mountains, its inland seas, its rivers and valleys, its hillsides and deep ravines; its winds and storms, the mystery of the desert, the wild beasts that stalk their prey and make inroads at times upon one's flocks. There is the vast sky overhead, the sun, the moon, and the stars; the light fading into darkness and coming again. There is regularity in nature and there is change. There is also the fact of death— the dying of nature after the season when animals have their young, or when the harvest is over; the death of the lowly creatures, life that one takes for his own food, and life that goes out for other reasons. There is the death of one's own kind, sometimes coming suddenly without warning, and again when one is full of years and ready to be gathered to his fathers. What is the effect upon one's thinking about

oneself when all these impressions and observations flood
in upon him? Are being born, managing one's household,
taking one's place in the world, loving, hating, fighting, and
dying all there is to human existence? Is there nothing beyond the thought of human extinction? To find answer to
these questions, one searches the myths and legends, stories
about the origins of things, how the earth and man came
to be. If one could know how everything started, one might
have the clue to all mysteries. One searches one's own mind,
puts together thoughts that have come from many sources,
and reflects on the future. Ultimately, what does it mean
to be man? That is the question which probes every event
in earth and sea and sky.

Out of all these questions, out of brooding on experiences, out of observations bearing on the way other people
live and think, one comes to conclusions about himself and
his race. One becomes conscious of himself as a being, not
merely as an agent. Meanings, hard won, are molded into
convictions that strengthen and undergird effort in maintaining oneself, warding off enemies, and enduring disasters.
The will to live becomes stronger than the fact of dying.
As the process goes on, one reaches the conclusion that there
is a distinctiveness about his life, a quality that sets him off
from others, a feeling that something very important is
bound up in him and his people, something that must never
perish. One comes to feel that living is not an affair of one's
own making. It is an event that happens to him. He feels
that he is not an accident, but is chosen for a mission that is
inescapable.

Once the meaning of this becomes clear, and one is convinced of its truth, it begins to pervade all acts. It becomes the reason for everything; all experiences are read in the light of a controlling purpose which provides explanation for origin and destiny and, through the understanding of these, gives direction to the present. Increasingly one feels that in his creation, there was a mandate to live in a certain way. In short, one is under the scrutiny of and subject to a Power greater than himself. Thinking in this way has the advantage of looking at all the diversities, contradictions, and tragedies of existence through a unity imposed upon them from without and which draws them to a center of meaning and purpose. Conclusions which one reaches, by inference from one's own observation or by inheritance from tradition, become beliefs. Supreme among these is the belief in God.

3. *God and the Soul*

The first fact about God that strikes us in the patriarchal period is the intimacy of His relationship with His people. His actions are reported in a pattern paralleling human behavior and ranging from the simplicity of a child's view of the world to the majesty of Sovereign Purpose. He walks in the garden in the cool of the day; He speaks and is heard; He calls Abraham and blesses him, promising a great future in a multitude of descendants through whom all the earth is to be blest. He opens the barren womb; He sends angels to talk to women who are puzzled about childbearing. Reticent about disclosing His name, His representatives come to Abraham's tent and eat the meal prepared for them. He goes down to see the cities of Sodom and Gomorrah so that he will know whether reports about them are true; He snatches Lot and his family from the doomed cities, taking them by the hand and leading them out; He sends fire and brimstone to destroy the wicked places. Before He does this, however, He feels under obligation to tell Abraham what He is going to do. He accepts Abraham's judgment that it would be wrong to destroy residents of the city who are righteous along with those who are wicked. He heeds Abraham's plea for Lot. When He finishes talking things over, He goes up to His place and Abraham goes to his. When Sarah denies that she laughed about having a son, the Lord contradicts her and tells her that she did laugh and adds, "Is anything too hard for the Lord?" In a dream, He threatens Abimelech with death for unwittingly taking Sarah from her husband, and demands that he restore her at once. He puts Abraham to the test by requiring the sacrifice of his only heir to the promise, and then recalls the command as the knife is raised to slay him on the altar. He reckons it for righteousness when Abraham believes Him. He inspires respect for Abraham among the neighbors and witnesses a covenant of mutual protection. He is especially careful about marriages because children are so important in perpetuating the purity of His purpose. He sends His angel to direct Abraham's servant in picking a wife for Isaac. He repeats all this concern in His dealings with Isaac, and makes him rich until he is envied by the neighbors.

At the birth of the twins, He chooses the younger to be the agent of His continuing purpose. He seems to enjoy the humor of Rebekah's plans to gain advantage for her favorite son, and her cleverness in outwitting her husband, and looks on Jacob's dealings with Laban with tacit approval and some reservations about the ethics of these affairs. He reminds Jacob of responsibilities which attend his favor and prosperity, and changes his name after putting him to the test in an all-night struggle on the banks of the Jabbok. Then He brings Jacob back to Bethel for a renewal of the covenant of his fathers. He allows Leah and her maid to give her husband a bounty of sons, and then chooses the son of Rachel, Joseph, for the main role in the critical days ahead. He takes sides in the rivalry of the brothers, and uses their evil plan to preserve the family and gain preference in the land of Pharaoh. He comforts the aging Jacob who is reluctant to leave his homeland by telling him that He will go with him to Egypt. He blesses the land of the Nile because Jacob and Joseph are there.

When the next crisis comes, the Lord meets it with a new leader equipped, for all his self-distrust, for the task of deliverance from Egyptian bondage. He hardens Pharaoh's heart, and then breaks it to show His power. He talks with Moses in the mountain. He listens to Moses' argument in behalf of the wayward people and yields to his plea. He reveals the law that is to be the foundation of the new nation. He imposes the discipline needed to transform slaves into responsible, free men. He becomes angry and shows His wrath. He evokes awe and reverence. He holds to His promise, chastises and forgives, for His own character is bound up in the history of this people. Yet, in spite of this persistent emphasis upon intimacy and mutuality, no injunction is more specific than the prohibition of images of the deity. Symbols of His presence, such as the Ark of the Covenant, the people may have. Sacred places, marking solemn promises and sacrifices, are legitimate means for sustaining devotion and regulating obedience to commandments, but the setting up of any visible likeness of God is forbidden above all else. This position, rooted in a conception of the being of God that does not allow even the revelation of His name, had decisive consequences in the spiritual pilgrimage of Israel. It is asserted before the whole world that ultimately the reality of God is established not by external signs and evidences but by inward intimacy with Him where He is known as the center and creator of unity in the soul. This is the burden which Hebrew man bore heroically amidst all vicissitude in bringing mankind to the maturity of personal autonomy.

During the period of the monarchy, the accessibility of God, His companionship and concern for the management of the nation, and His power over events continue with only those modifications which arise out of the necessities of a new setting. The fear of losing distinctiveness emerges with the kingship of Saul, and recurs throughout the later history. As the tribes consolidate into a nation, and enemies are quieted on the borders, the sense of solidarity takes on new dimensions in a quickened feeling of realization. A transition, however, is under way from the kind of personal relation between the patriarchs and God to a representative relationship through certain especially qualified individuals. The older type of intimacy is not lost, but increasingly the priest and the prophet assume the functions of mediator and interpreter of the will of God. This transfer of responsibility to official guardians of the cultus also opens the way for more use by the masses of the local deities on the high places. It is in this sort of setting that the later prophets emerge to make powerful appeal for the recovery of the earlier intimacy in the dimension of new events which disclose a view of the meaning of God in history that reaches beyond the bounds of the nation in universal service.

Thus it turns out that the God of Israel is a god whose nature and power are peculiarly suited to crisis as a means of carrying on His creation in man. This is so because it is in crisis that older structures of living are shattered, and the soul is compelled to make new ones to serve the new demands. With the national existence ended, the prophets, by judgment based on what has happened and by proffer of hope based on future promise of obedience, open the way to a spiritual renaissance. The key to their insight is the rediscovery of the individual in a mode of self-consciousness that combines freedom and responsibility in conscience. In the final analysis, it is at the inward junction of right and wrong that God meets man. The capacity to create good by choice is what makes man the image of God. This basic reality must never be clouded by any form of idolatry in which rite and ceremony stifle the vitality of decision and dull sensitivity to the fact of human solidarity. In his review of history, the author of one of the documents of the Old Testament rewrites the story of creation (Genesis 1:1-2a) showing that it was the Spirit of God that in the beginning moved upon chaos to create the heavens and the earth, man and all the rest, assigning to each creature his character, place, and function on the basis of differentiation and peculiar character. The beginning is joined with the ending in affirming that being true to oneself, holding to integrity according to the purpose of God, all diversions to the contrary notwithstanding, is the essence of the divine revelation in the soul of Israel. Implications beyond this require attention in concluding this chapter.

4. *The Prophets and Believing Man*

The writing prophets bring us to the summit of the development of religion in Israel and to further understanding of the nature of the internal life of man. Thus far we have pursued our purpose in a sequence of events which, in the character of a particular people acting in roles adapted to their times, presented a variety of insights into human nature. In simple paraphrasing of significant portions of the record, we have studied the soul of Israel on its own terms and used familiar concepts and modes of interpretation to give structure and direction to our thought. These must now be reviewed briefly and related to the remaining issue before us in the Old Testament setting.

We began with self-consciousness as the distinctive mark of man and described it as the capacity of the human being to stand clear of himself, to perceive the meaning of his own existence and undertake the direction of life through loyalty to a purpose beyond self. Now we ask, What is involved in the act of self-consciousness? What kind of event is it? By what means does it occur as a state of being? To probe the question further, what is the import of those reflexive pronouns which fall so easily from our lips without notice of what they say, though they are the very stuff of us? Myself, yourself, herself, himself, and their appropriate plurals—why do we need them? The most obvious implication of these words is the feeling of possession that pervades them. This leads to the question, Who owns the self, *my* self? Who is recognized in the reference to *your* self? Likewise, who is the subject of the object "him" and "her" in the other words? What is the event in the sentence, "He must do it *himself*"? An idiomatic way of stressing that the act contemplated must be initiated and carried through in a manner peculiar to *him*? Yes, but plainly there is more to the thought than that. He, in his acting is expressing command over an instrument, the body-mind self, through which *he* as a whole affects nature and society.

In this context, we face explicitly what has been with us all along in our study of the soul of Israel and would be with us in the study of any other soul. The second major component of the internal life now appears in clear light. The biosocial self is under the direction of the *person*. The self, in aspects of body and mind and composed of social experiences held together in a unity, is *it*. The person is *he*, possessing, using, changing the self. The word "self-conscious" conceals the main psychic event unless it is understood that the act of consciousness is made possible by the unique character of individual reaction to internalized social experience. In our previous discussion, we have repeatedly used the phrase "being true to itself" when referring to the sense of obligation in the soul of Israel. Now we see that the statement requires the added fact that the soul cannot be true to itself except as it becomes fully the person. Our gain, then, at this point, consists in seeing together the components of the soul—self and person—in their psychological character. A more precise examination of this character must be left to a later chapter. It remains for us to consider here the contribution of the prophets to our understanding of personhood.

When we speak of the person as the internal reaction of the individual to social experience and examine the grounds for distinguishing it from the self, we observe again the process of recapitulation and transcendence. The interaction of the body-mind self with other selves is facilitated by the human capacity for speech—language, communication. In each experience of such interaction, the impressions which one makes upon another are reflected back to him in gestures and words. He comes to know who he is by the accumulative responses of others as they are conserved in verbal symbols and further reacted to in modes of accepting, rejecting, adapting. Such activity is the mark of the person and makes possible the inward dialogue through which a man may relive his past and reshape it in the presence of the demands of each new situation that confronts him. The work of the prophets illustrates this tendency at a high level in two issues with which we close the Old Testament section of our study.

First, the prophets looked upon failure, suffering, crisis, as incentives for new adventure in the onward march of Israel toward the fulfillment of her mission. When the foundations of the nation as self crumbled forever, they rose in the dignity of man's autonomy as person. Is there in any literature a more magnificent scene than the one portrayed in Jeremiah 32 where the prophet, at the moment of utter national desolation, goes to Anathoth, buys a field, has the transaction certified by the legal procedure of a state *continuing in power,* and proclaims with conviction unsupported by external event: "Houses and fields and vineyards shall again be bought in the land"? Matching this, with moving eloquence, is the Second Isaiah's vision of the world mission of Israel as the Servant of the Lord, an outcome not explicit in the call to Abraham but a transformation and an unanticipated fulfillment of it accomplished by the rigorous discipline of a baffling history. In this, the soul of Israel emerges in its highest form by affirming responsibility not merely for self but for the destiny of mankind. The figure of the Servant is Israel acting as person.

In addition to this, the prophets help us to understand the specific content of that aspect of the soul which we have called the person. As the term itself implies, man lives by words, by beliefs formulated in propositions accepted as true. The life of the person, indeed, exists in attitudes and beliefs. These may be seen operating in all human affairs.

Wherever a man goes, he uses attitudes for "taking hold" of the situation before him. By beliefs, he knows himself, is known by others, defines his position and directs his action. The prophets, with conscience sharpened to discern righteousness and proclaim it, lived by the power of words as did Moses when he stood before Pharaoh. Above all, there was for them a supreme Word, the Word of the Lord. They got their name from this fact. In communicating the judgment, mercy, and love of God, they reflected back to Israel her own soul transformed, and, in that act, sought to make clear man's image of himself as the likeness of his Creator. Thus, in a relationship which we may now express by *me-I-Thou*—self, person, God—the prophets bring us, in the latter years, to the vision of human fulfillment in personhood.

4. FULFILLMENT—JESUS

THE HISTORY OF ISRAEL BEGAN WITH A PROMISE sealed by a covenant in which God and His people are conceived as one in working out a common purpose. In the preceding chapters, we have observed how that undertaking advanced through succeeding settings or situations which required the renewal of inward strength to meet the challenge of external threats. In the early period, the movement took root and was carried forward by the action of individual patriarchs. In the second, under Moses, it took the form of national aspirations issuing in the final settlement of Canaan and the establishment of the monarchy. In the third, marked by the disillusionment of the nation and the emergence of the great prophets, it took the form of a religious community whose final formal act was the canonization of the Jewish scriptures—first the Pentateuch, then, some centuries later, the Prophets and the Writings.

In each of these steps whose limits we have set somewhat arbitrarily, there was a recapitulation of the past, a return to essentials, and a reorientation toward the future. The

119

central fact is that the original purpose did not perish. External attack, internal dissension and apostasy, thwarted, but did not stop, the soul of Israel in its onward march. It exhibited remarkable capacity for creative adaptation, for self-acceptance in changed circumstances, and for reaffirmation of faith in its mission. It learned how "to mount up with wings like eagles," how "to run and not be weary," how "to walk and not faint." No event in the history of Israel ever led to a total loss; and in time every event was seen to provide some gain that guaranteed survival and made life worth living. Resiliency and toughness, capacity to concede with reassertion of demand, kept the soul in the stream of history. These qualities were especially manifest during the two centuries immediately preceding the Christian era.

Two major developments, not treated in the Old Testament, took place during this period. One was the movement known as the Hellenization of Western Asia and Egypt after the sweeping conquests of Alexander and the continuance of Greek power and influence under the Seleucids, whose dynasty extended from 363-312 B.C. The outstanding literary result of this cultural interpenetration was the translation of the Jewish scriptures into the Greek known as the Septuagint. This was the "Bible" of the Jews of the Dispersion and of the early Christians. The second historic event was the occupation of West Asia by the Romans, a task which was completed a little more than a half century before Christ.

These encroachments upon Jewish life and institutions

were met, for the most part, by attempts at accommodation, and by open, defiant resistance when pagan arrogance became intolerable. A conspicuous example of the latter was the revolt led by the Maccabees against Antiochus IV (Epiphanes), king of Syria from 176-164 B.C. This ruler heaped upon the Jews unbearable indignities. When he authorized sacrifice to Zeus on the altar of Yahweh in Jerusalem, the entire nation, including those who had become advocates of Hellenism, was outraged. The priestly house of the Maccabees, known also by the ancestral name as Hasmoneans, led first by its head, Mattathias, and later by his sons, Judas, Jonathan, and Simon, rallied forces for armed rebellion. The spirit of nationalism revived with an intensity which swept through successive stages to a victory for political and religious autonomy that lasted nearly thirty years. The Feast of Dedication, Hanukkah, instituted at the rededication of the Second Temple in this period, marked a memorable triumph which provided encouragement for sporadic outbreaks against foreign powers in subsequent years. The coming of the Romans continued the pattern established by the Greeks and offered, at best, only alternatives of desperation.

In these troubled times, the soul of Israel underwent deep, inward travail, in some respects more galling than the ravages of the Assyrians and Babylonians. Under the heel of enemies who combined military might with mild tolerance for the religious peculiarities of conquered peoples, and who relied upon cultural infiltration to accomplish what brute force could not, the Jews were sorely pressed.

Often they were embarrassed by their own sacred traditions. Unfailingly, they renewed their trust in Yahweh, confident that He would intervene in their behalf. They remembered the mighty acts of Moses and the miraculous deliverance of Jerusalem from the army of Sennacherib in the time of Hezekiah. In consequence, resort to arms was looked upon as a measure required by extreme conditions, or as the final pledge of faithfulness. Strict observance of the Sabbath offered the enemy special advantage in planning his attack on the day of rest and worship. The dietary laws also provided occasion for humiliation at the hands of the insensitive foreigner. In I Maccabees (1:62), there is a reference to the firm resolve of the Jews not to eat food forbidden by the code of holiness and, in II Maccabees (7:1), we are told how shameless the enemy was in forcing a group of them to eat "swine's flesh."

Nevertheless, all the forms of degradation visited upon the people were met with a courage and a faith which combined to produce one of the spiritual monuments of history. Among all the conquered races, the Jews were peculiarly equipped to survive the test to which they were subjected. First and foremost, was the fact that they had always acknowledged the claims of a sovereignty above earthly rulers, including their own kings. When, therefore, they had no visible head, they continued to exist as a religious community with Yahweh as their supreme and unchanging sovereign. Under duress of conditions repugnant to their beliefs and practices, they found refuge and strength in an inward citadel which no enemy could enter. The Psalms which were written during this period attest this with moving eloquence. But the main secret is found in two mutually related centers of loyalty which sustained them in their ordeal—the Law or Torah, and the Temple. These were the visible and vocal signs of Yahweh's presence and power, and they were defended with unflagging zeal. Acts of violence or desecration, directed toward the Torah or the House of the Lord, evoked the strongest protest. Canny stratagem was devised to outwit the intruder. Martyrdom snatched the power of the sword from the hand of him who drew it to kill the body but could not touch the spirit.

But this did not in any sense mean pure passivity. By the end of the period which we are discussing, various sects or parties had come into existence with proposals for remedying the current evils. In the time of Joshua, the Hellenist who called himself Jason, in order to be in good style as a Greek, the Hasidim (the Pious) arose to counteract the Hellenistic tendency among the Jews. Later, this sect divided into the Pharisees and Essenes. Others, such as the Sadducees and Zealots, expressed differing convictions concerning proper methods for dealing with the situation confronting them. Sustaining all effort, however, were two other influences of important consequence. One was the apocalyptic writings, like the Book of Daniel, which rendered the judgments of Yahweh upon the enemy within the gates and encouraged the faithful by the vision of ultimate deliverance. Above all, the supremacy of the Torah gave rise to a vast rabbinical literature which interpreted it and applied it to the most minute details of daily living. This much

needed guidance in a time of confusion was the work of
the Scribes. Conspicuously absent, throughout the entire
period, was the voice of a commanding prophet. But he, in
a form undreamed of, was destined to come.

1. *Adventure Unbounded*

On opening the pages of the New Testament, we know at
once that we are in the midst of scenes where age-old tendencies of human nature reappear to encounter a power of
the spirit equal to their challenge, and to set the fact of
religious self-consciousness in its final form. Standing at
this point in history, we look back over a thousand years.
We see the procession of advancing and retreating armies of
powerful eastern neighbors, alternately subduing and surrendering Palestine, and offering periodic respites for re-
cuperation and the gaining of a new hold on existence.
Finally we hear the thud of marching Greeks and Romans.

With all this before our minds, it is breath-taking to
realize that it was in those days that Jesus came preaching.
It is as though a stage were set in magnificent drama, each
act and scene moving forward with increasing complication
of the plot until the point is reached where all hope for
resolution of the issues fades. Then with unassuming ease
and majestic mastery, the hero enters for a climax that reacts upon all that has gone before and transforms the whole
in one grand act of fulfillment. If anyone doubts the reality
of purpose in the world, centering upon the total destiny
of mankind, he needs only to see this fact in its actual his-

toric dimensions. The purpose is explicit in the events, unfolding then retreating from sight, coming again on the mountain of prophetic vision, then dying back to come alive at last in a living revelation that unites the freedom of man with the purpose of God in unforgettable words and deeds. It is a startling, staggering fact that this happened, that a little plot of earth, scarcely ten thousand acres in area, was the crucible in which, by fire and sword, by siege of greed and hate, the soul of man, in the fullness of love and wisdom, should at last come into full view of heaven and earth. The record proclaims without equivocation that this did happen! "In many and various ways God spoke of old to our fathers by the prophets; but in these last days he has spoken to us by a Son." [1]

In Jesus the soul of Israel achieves final emancipation from blood and soil, and is installed with power as Pioneer in the universal quest for personhood. In him it became possible for the whole world to perceive what first came to light in the previous age—that there is one God and he is the God of all people—a fact which makes all peoples one. The fullness of this fact could not appear until actually the East and the West found a meeting point; until in a particular time and place, all the elements of the human in history could come together in the mind of one prepared individual and, in him, be shaped by a divine act which made the total history a revelation. It is then that time marks an era and a new day dawns.

---

[1] Hebrews 1:1,2. (RSV)

When we read the Gospels of the New Testament, we know that we are looking at Jesus through the eyes of his loyal followers. He himself left no written word. Moreover, what the record contains is a part of the effort of the early preachers to communicate his message to others who occupied a social, political, and religious situation that offered other alternatives for solving the problems of the time. It is the aim of those who remembered him and his words to convince their contemporaries that Jesus is the one above all others in whom they should put their faith, that in and through him, the supreme assurance of salvation is to be found.

In other words, just as the developing self-consciousness in Israel during the period of the monarchy gave rise to the impulse to collect and put together the traditions, myths, and legends, bearing on the origin and destiny of the Hebrew people, so in the latter half of the first century A.D., the followers of Jesus, now bound together in a religious community, began to look back upon his earthly career to discern what he had said and done in order to relate it to the needs of men in their time and undergird the church as an agency of redemption. This retrospection, however, did not center upon the nation but upon a person whose internal character enabled him to act in every human situation with divine courage, freedom, and power.

We learn about Jesus, then, through the attempt of his followers to evoke faith in him and to secure personal commitment to the movement which he had started and which they believed would ultimately lead to the consummation of the purpose to which he had given his life. Though it is natural that we should wish for a pure biography of Jesus, there is probably nothing more characteristic of his inward certitude than his lack of interest in setting down his own words or setting up an organization designed deliberately to perpetuate his influence. The course of events in the particulars of the early Christian community was not foreseen or dictated by him, but it was in accord with his inmost secret, as we shall see, that it should be left to time and occasion. His own view of his mission, and the method he chose to fulfill it, made this practically inevitable.

2. *The Miracle of Trust in God*

What was the secret of Jesus? What was the conviction on which he staked everything? In regard to other questions about him and his teaching, there may be room for doubt and controversy, but to these we have an unqualified, authentic answer. It is clear beyond the shadow of any doubt that Jesus felt so at one with God, so completely united with the divine will that he put his trust in God without reservation. This is the paramount and pervasive element in all his acts, the one thing needful, both from his point of view and from ours. To make the meaning of this trust real to his followers was his constant aim and all the variations in their reports about him do not at any point obscure this fact. Though they may have misunderstood him in regard to other matters, and though this, the main one, was hard to live by, they transmitted it with a clarity beyond possibility of misunderstanding.

Once the total picture is before us, we can discern in clear outline the central figure in it and, notwithstanding the shading of the apostolic colors, we see the source of the power which made him what he was in uncorrupted integrity. Discovering this, we know also why it was so difficult to follow him, why through the centuries that difficulty has never been overcome, why now we still follow him afar off, why we plead for some occasion "beyond history" to actualize his will.[2] For all the fine approximations to his ideal during the centuries since, no one has ever trusted God the way he did. That is the miracle of the ages *par excellence*! It is before that fact, more than any other, that we feel the burden of our own human nature. With this key to the Gospels, we may look at some of the passages in which the great truth emerges.

The career of Jesus belonged naturally in the framework of Judaism. Although he cannot be explained by this fact alone, it is impossible, in so far as we may look for any explanation, to imagine him appearing in any other cultural and religious setting of ancient times. It would prob-

---

[2] It is the character of Jesus' trust in God, its depth and constancy, as the unifying and controlling element in all occasions, that makes the quality of his thought transcend the eschatological view of history in the very act of using that view. Indeed, trust in God, in the dimensions of his faith, is a view of history that rises above all other views. It is an inward union of immediate and ultimate event which makes the demarcation of temporal occasions, *chronos,* mere legerdemain, useful but relatively inconsequential. Furthermore, this trust in God is an act in truth which is not subject to change in world views.

ably not be true to say that the history of Israel looked to his coming in a definitive sense in that it required such a consummation, but it can be said that all the antecedents which shape the self-consciousness of Jesus are in the religion which he inherited with, of course, in addition, his own unique reaction to the times in which he lived. In such terms, he is not unlike the prophets before him, but he is more than a prophet. His loyalty to the faith of his fathers is not to be questioned, but his experience of the world of his day, his contact as Galilean with non-Jewish culture, the striking fact of the universal Roman empire stirring the imagination to envision a kingdom of God along lines consonant with, but having character and dimensions different from Judaism, are all elements *in* his outlook, but not *of* it.

Assuming the basic conviction which we have suggested as indicating his conception of himself and his mission, it was natural for Jesus to look for an appropriate starting point. That was available in the work of John the baptizer. This man, with some of the characteristics of Elijah, lived in the wilderness bordering the Jordan. He was attracting people by a forthright challenge to get ready for a new age. Probably there were many voices like his in those times when religious and nationalistic aspirations often ran high, but John was taken seriously because of the specific demands which he made upon those who came to him. He had such assurance about the coming event that he urged the people to respond to his message by definite acts of participation in it. He announced judgment on the sins of the

age and practiced a baptism of repentance. This baptism
was not a mere rite of purification in the Jewish sense of
its use, nor was it just a symbol of inner change. It was an
act which connected the individual with the change itself.
Jesus shared this conviction of John and joined himself to
the movement by accepting the baptism. In doing so, his
conception of himself was intensified, and this led to a testing and a decision concerning his future role. Consequently
he is ready to begin his active ministry when the signal
comes in the imprisonment of John. His first utterance
sounds the note that recurs in every subsequent word and
act. "The time is fulfilled, and the kingdom of God is at
hand; repent, and believe in the gospel." [3] These words
mean what they say. Paraphrasing them, they announce,
"The kingdom is here now with me. This is the good news.
Believe it. Put out of your minds everything that prevents
your acceptance of this fact." Later when John sends messengers to inquire of Jesus whether he is the one who was
to come, Jesus gives answer in terms that are consonant
with this initial proclamation. He does not specifically iden-
tify himself to John, but draws attention to the evidence—
the blind see, the lame walk, and the poor have the gospel
preached to them. It is enough, for these activities mean
that God is showing His power in Jesus in such a way as to
bring in the new day. The point becomes even clearer in the
specific acts of healing as they occur from time to time. In
the curing of the paralytic, one of the chief prerogatives of

---

[3] Mark 1:15. (RSV)

God—forgiveness—is equated with taking up the pallet and walking. To say, "Thy sins are forgiven," or to be healed, expresses the same fact. The power of God is manifest in the work of Jesus. Even more specific is Jesus' answer to the charge that he cast out demons by the aid of Beelzebul, so, "If it is by the finger of God that I cast out demons, then the kingdom of God has come unto you." [4]

In matters touching the law, Jesus expresses the view that its original purpose was to serve the needs of men. He does not hesitate to act in disregard to the interpretations in the "traditions of the elders" because the presence of God, who gave it in the beginning, warrants modifications required by the demands of the particular situation. His sense of God's immediacy and companionship justifies his action in allowing his disciples to pluck the heads of grain to satisfy their hunger on the Sabbath and in healing the man with the withered hand in the synagogue. "The Son of man is Lord also of the sabbath." [5] Likewise his disciples do not fast when it is inappropriate to do so. Unless there exists an occasion to which the act is a genuine response, one becomes involved in unreality and hypocrisy. The same holds true with respect to ceremonial washing, for it is not what enters into a man that defiles him, but what comes out of him. It is what really expresses the spirit and attitude of the heart that counts before God.

It was the divine intention in giving the law that an

---

[4] Luke 11:20. (RSV)
[5] Mark 2:28.

unselfish spirit would thereby be guaranteed, but if in the application of the law the interests of the poor, the distressed, the "little ones," are not served, God stands ready to intervene directly in their behalf. It is not His will that one of these should perish. A cup of cold water to a thirsty man is a deed that has its reward. It is not by striving for the chief seats in the future kingdom that one attains divine approval, but by readiness to act now as servant of God in meeting the needs of His children. This indeed is what the Son of Man came to do. He is before you, and in him you see works which are the equivalent of God acting.

In essence, this is the meaning of all that Jesus does. His acts are to be viewed as evidence of the direct, immediate invasion of human life by the spirit of God with far-reaching consequences for transforming the total world order. God can start anywhere in remaking man. His activity is not limited to special auspices, set up by men, no matter how precise and how reverent the cultus that is designed to relate men to the divine purpose may be. Like the prophets before him, Jesus sees the peril of putting such emphasis on rule and ritual that the interests of the common man are subverted, that the institution defining approach to God may actually shut Him out from the worshiper or, by subtlety, result in actual violation of the commandment of God.[6]

Even more positive is the emphasis of Jesus on the individual and his capacity to respond to the will of God.

---

[6] Mark 7:10-13.

He begins by announcing the fact of God's concern for all men regardless of their class or condition.

> Blessed are you poor. . . .
> Blessed are you that hunger now. . . .
> Blessed are you that weep now. . . .
> Blessed are you when men hate you. . . .
> Rejoice in that day and leap for joy . . . ;
>   for so their fathers did to the prophets.[7]

These words are addressed to people who are surrounded on every side by overwhelming worldly power in whose interests they are taxed and who are subjected to all manner of exploitation. In their helplessness, Jesus speaks to them about resources directly available to them in God if they will turn to Him with their whole heart. His logic seems to be that the presence of desperation is the very occasion for God to manifest Himself. In another context Amos saw an act of God in the approaching armies of Assyria. In this new situation, when the individual is thrown back upon himself, God is there with power to meet his need and will use the person's response creatively to establish His kingdom. The supreme barrier to entrance into the kingdom is unbelief, lack of trust. It was to break through this barrier that Jesus engaged in his healing work. It demonstrated that when all hope seems gone, when men are without resources in themselves, an act of faith will break through to a discovery of strength unknown before. In the light of such a possibility, Jesus can say, "Blessed are you." It is not the condition it-

---

[7] Luke 6:20-23. (RSV)

self that he acclaims, but the opportunity it presents for the transformation of man the self, into man the person, by the power of faith in God.

But there are other obstacles to faith even more resistant than disease, for they seem to have such solid, implacable substance. Chief among these is riches. Attachment to wealth with the power that goes along with it has always been a peculiar property of human nature. It is related to self-maintenance and security and seems to provide an adequate solution to every problem. It is capable also of becoming man's supreme goal and the root of all his motivations. When it attains that position in life, it becomes idolatry and stands opposed to God. Emperor worship in Jesus' time was a conspicuous example of what can happen when men make riches and power their aim; hence the necessity of a clear decision, a complete renunciation.

Ye cannot serve God and mammon.[8]

Lay not up for yourselves treasures upon earth. . . .[9]

These things are transient, easily taken away, and if you put your trust in them, you may be left stranded and helpless at any moment, especially in troublous times. "Go, sell what you have, and give to the poor . . . then come, follow me."[10] "It is easier for a camel to go through the eye of a needle than for a rich man to enter the kingdom of God."[11]

---

[8] Matthew 6:24.
[9] Matthew 6:19.
[10] Mark 10:21. (RSV)
[11] Mark 10:25. (RSV)

"Thou fool, this night thy soul shall be required of thee." [12]

Faith in the kingdom warrants selling all one has, like the pearl merchant who disposed of his total stock in order that he might purchase the superb pearl; or it is like the man who sold everything in order that he might buy a field that contained a rich treasure. Things, as useful as they may be, are deceiving because they seem to offer so much and soon become so empty of power. It is the soul only that has value before God. "What shall it profit a man if he gain the whole world," like Caesar, "and lose his own soul?" All these things in which men so easily put their trust are barriers to faith and must be renounced. There can be no equivocating, no compromise. The decision must be radical and complete. It seems impossible, but, "with God, all things are possible." He will not stop short of completing His creation in man. Trust Him. Do not be anxious. Seek first the kingdom in the integrity of inward motive. What you need will be added.

Jesus' teaching concerning the immediacy of the kingdom in him, and its future realization, appears also in other parables which present the reasons for faith and choice balancing the warnings that call for renunciation. A strong note of encouragement is given in the parable of the seed that is sown and left alone. The two crucial statements are, "the earth produces of itself" and "the harvest has come." [13] It is not the process of the growth that is central, but the certainty, the inevitability of the kingdom. The parable of

---

[12] Luke 12:20.
[13] Mark 4:28, 29. (RSV)

the leaven in the dough further stresses this. Likewise a small beginning will issue in great accomplishment as the grain of mustard seed; or produce as much as a hundredfold if the soil is good. The evidence of God's presence is inescapable, so clear, in fact, that the discerning can judge it as easily as they interpret the signs of the weather, the coming of spring in the putting forth of leaves of the fig tree in anticipation of the fruit immediately to follow.

Of special importance are those parables which disclose more specifically Jesus' conception of God and the intimacy of his own inward relationship to Him. In the parable of the laborers in the vineyard, where the man who worked only one hour received the same wage as those who had worked longer, it is made clear that man's effort to achieve righteousness does not decisively condition God's response, for His grace is equally available to all. Membership in the kingdom is not earned; it is a gift that comes through trust. In the stories of the lost, those who are personally estranged from current religion and find it inadequate to meet their needs evoke the direct concern of God whose outreach toward them expresses a constant readiness to bestow His favor. When they turn to Him, Jesus indicates the exuberant joy of God in receiving them. In the inimitable story of the lost son and his brother, the description of God's grace, His unqualified forgiveness and love are presented in most moving terms.

In all his teaching about God, Jesus unites in his own heart awareness of human frailty on the one hand and complete assurance of the presence and power of God on the other. In him, the kingdom has truly come, is in the midst of the people now, and even though men are unable to respond fully because of their involvement in affairs of this world, such faith as they can manifest is guarantee of a joyous consummation in the future. God is so real to Jesus, his trust in Him is so complete, his certainty of the ultimate triumph of the divine will for man so unqualified, that he can view it as a fact already accomplished. This conviction issues naturally and spontaneously in his self-estimate as Son of Man, and enables him to face all obstacles—the inertia and blindness of the multitudes, the opposition of official religion, and the pagan dullness of Roman power—with unwavering faith. When he presses for a decision in going up to Jerusalem in the last days, it is already settled in his mind what his attitude will be. The outcome is entirely in the hands of God. If the answer is "Not now," or if it is "Yes, but not in this way," Jesus' assurance will remain unchanged. No one, not even the Son of Man, knows the hour, and it is not necessary for him to yield to the signs of "Lo here" or "Lo there." Such was the strength of his unbounded faith in God and, to confirm it, he needed no more response from men than that expressed in his simile about the grain of mustard seed.

3. *Solidarity with Men*

Notwithstanding all that God can and will do, Jesus accepts his full part in the establishment of the kingdom even to the point of surrendering his life. The corollary of this act is the obligation and necessity for his disciples to do the same, for they are the first citizens of the kingdom. Through their witness, the new life is to be commended to the world. They must live their faith in God. They must be doers of the word, not hearers only. Jesus is speaking, of course, to them as individuals. He shares the hopes of his people, variously expressed by them in nationalistic and apocalyptic terms but, in the total perspective of his outlook, his attitude makes room for "other sheep, not of this fold." It is the kingdom in whatever form God may choose to establish it that lies at the center of his faith. He is living that faith now in the reality of God in his own life, and it should be emphasized that his view of this working of God is no delusion. The painstaking care with which he sought to make his message clear to his disciples, his attitude toward the sick, his belief in their spiritual capacity, no matter what their station or condition might be, are impressive evidence that what he is asking, though difficult to act upon, is within the range of possibility for all men.

It must never be forgotten that Jesus' sense of his own relationship to God carries with it inevitably an affirmation of confidence in men. In his own self-affirmation before God, he acknowledges his association with men, his involvement in the issues of life in this world, and his belief that those whom he has called from the most humble ranks of his day can become his true followers. His whole ministry was predicated upon this twofold faith without which his faith in himself would have been impossible. Indeed, had it not included his fellow men, he would have died a "mental case" or disappeared among the pious folk like the Essenes. There is in Jesus a stern discipline of the spirit, but no cynicism or withdrawal from society. He does not adopt the method of John the baptizer although he approved of the aims of that movement. From the beginning he knows that the issues before him must be thought out openly, face to face with the men of his day, for these issues are theirs and he believes that if they can see them clearly they will act in the measure of God's expectation of them. In his own origin, he is of the common folk, a carpenter. He is intimately identified with the aspirations of the rank and file. He does not belong to the school of the prophets, nor has he been trained by the rabbinate in Jerusalem. His choice of the fishermen, his association with publicans and sinners, and his love of children, reveal his sense of the primacy of spontaneous, uninhibited response to God in the actual situations of the common life. His compassion for the oppressed and the weak is the very essence of a normality that continues to be a basic quality of his character during all the days of his extraordinary mission.

The final proof of all this is seen in the seriousness with which he laid on his followers the obligations of membership in the kingdom. His demands are supported by genuine encouragement, but they are stated in the most explicit and exacting terms. The chief and overarching requirement is love. In all their relationships this is to be the key to inner attitude and action, for it is by love that men are to be fitted for the kingdom. The law and the prophets are summed up in wholehearted love toward God and loving one's neighbor as oneself. The logic of this is very simple. Unity of purpose with God is inseparable from solidarity with one's fellow men. One's self-evaluation as a child of God is the norm by which one discerns the value of other men, and is able to relate himself to them in brotherhood. This love is like that of the Samaritan rescuer of the man who fell among thieves on the road to Jericho and was left half dead. It is no sentimental philanthropy. It is the gracious outgoing of a warm heart to a fellow human being whose dignity and worth are at stake. It is an act freed from the dictates of a formal religion which has prescriptions of routine for doing good. This love is manifest in a spirit of forgiveness that outruns the rule of "seven times" and becomes "seventy times seven." It transforms the compulsion to go one mile into the privilege and adventure of going the second. It regulates one's attitude toward one's enemies. It counsels losing one's life in unselfish service as the way of finding it.

These demands upon his disciples, far from depreciating human capacity, represent an extraordinary confidence in it, and when they are told that the importance of these matters is greater than going home to bury one's father, or to look after one's business, it is clear that Jesus believes his followers can, by the discipline of the narrow gate, attain unto a spiritual stature not unlike his own, though that is now far removed from them. If he said, "You must be perfect as your heavenly father is perfect," he certainly meant it, and that at least implies that one's best approximation to what God expects is sufficient to allow His grace to do the rest. The authority for this new life flows through trust, and its final test is its fruits.

Such, in briefest compass, was the ministry of Jesus and his disclosure of the meaning of the adventure of personality on this planet. In him we see human nature in union with God, the fulfillment or actualization of what is in man as personal possibility. The significance of Jesus in human history has been attested by thousands who, through the centuries, have sought to understand him and follow him. But probably no one, outside the main stream of formal theology, has more aptly appraised his mind and teaching than a distinguished modern philosopher, Alfred North Whitehead, who wrote more than a quarter of a century ago the following words:

> The reported sayings of Christ are not formularized thought. They are descriptions of direct insight. The ideas are in his mind as immediate pictures, and not as analyzed in terms of abstract concepts. He sees intuitively the relations between good men and bad men; his expressions are not cast in the form of an analysis of the goodness and badness of man. His sayings are actions and not adjustments of concepts. He speaks in the lowest abstractions that language is capable of if it is to be language at all and not the fact itself.
>
> In the Sermon on the Mount and in the parables, there is no reasoning about the facts. They are seen with immeasurable innocence. Christ represents rationalism derived from direct intuition and divorced from dialectics.
>
> The life of Christ is not an exhibition of overruling power. Its glory is for those who can discern it and not

for the world. Its power lies in its absence of force. It has the decisiveness of a supreme ideal, and that is why the history of the world divides at this point of time.[14]

In the perspective in which we see Jesus as the culmination of the religious process of the Old Testament, we may conclude by saying that in him the soul of Israel attained full integrity of self-consciousness through the realization of that intimacy with God which had been the vital breath of faith from Abraham to the last of the great prophets, one of whom dared to say:

> Behold, the days are coming, says the Lord, when I will make a new covenant with the house of Israel and the house of Judah, not like the covenant which I made with their fathers. . . . But this is the covenant which I will make . . . : I will put my law within them, and I will write it upon their hearts; and I will be their God, and they shall be my people.[15]

Thus, through him, the singular religious genius, which had been developed in Israel by centuries of struggle and suffering, was at last universalized as a creative and redemptive force among the peoples of the western world. But, in this, his life was more than a fulfillment of events and a response to a new historical situation. He achieved an inner autonomy which was neither determined nor bound by external occasion. His relations with the world were trans-

---

[14] Alfred North Whitehead. *Religion in the Making*, pp. 56, 57. New York: The Macmillan Company, 1926. Used by permission of the publisher.

[15] Jeremiah 31:31-33. (RSV)

formed by decisions grounded in his trust in God and these, taken in the composite of his words and deeds, disclosed that transcendence of self which set for all time the goal of man's search for true personhood.

5. TRANSITION—PAUL

IN OUR STUDY OF THE ADVENTURE OF PERSONALITY in the Bible, we have observed that in each period or setting of events, the soul of Israel exhibits the tendency to recapitulate the past, selectively to gather up essential elements related to origins, meanings, and destiny and, in adaptation to a changed situation, emerges with differences that set the stage for subsequent development. This is to say, in effect, that history is a succession of events in which activities of the objective world of nature and of men evoke subjective responses that reshape these events in the presence of new demands. It is thus that the internal life becomes the agent of history and in so far as the effort at any time attempts to achieve a wholeness through establishing connections between God, man, and the world, it is a distinctively religious enterprise. The meaning of the word religion itself conveys this essential fact—a binding back of all diversities of experience into unity, into God as creator and fundamental ground of existence.

This phenomenon reappears in Saul of Tarsus, or Paul

as he came to be known. Judaism, in its later form, mediating the patriarchal, Mosaic, and prophetic elements, provides the basic outlook for his life and thought. In the final results, however, he passes beyond the bounds of the faith in which he was nurtured and educated in the school of Gamaliel. He gives us explicit information about the position which he occupied in relation to the religious tradition in which he was born and to the early Christian movement. He belonged to the tribe of Benjamin and was a Pharisee of the strictest kind. In loyalty to his religious inheritance, his zeal was unsurpassed. One of the chief marks of this devotion was his intense opposition to all rivals of Judaism. His first contact with the "Christians" was a determined attempt to wipe them out. The record states that he witnessed the stoning of Stephen with a more positive interest than that of a bystander. He himself reports that he persecuted the church of God and harried it. His own words and the tradition in The Acts attest to the violence of his attacks.

Yet all this was reversed, and he became not only an ardent believer in the faith he had sought to destroy, but also its most vigorous and undaunted apostle with an intellectual gift for reconstructing it that made him a power to conjure with through succeeding centuries. How this happened, next to the account of the career of Jesus in the Gospels, is the big story of the first century A.D. Our present interest centers in the person of Paul and his vocation. To us, his career is a remarkable adventure combining intellectual power, under drive of intense emotional conflict,

with large responsibility for practical action. In him the
dynamics of human nature surge and seethe, flash and
flame, ranging in mood from the depths to the heights or
striking balance in between, as reason gropes for order and
faith steers a steady course. We shall look first at his work
as a thinker in the light of his relationship to early Chris-
tianity.

1. *Resurrection and Rebirth*

Paul's lack of personal contact with Jesus has been a subject
of constant inquiry by students of the early church. Their
careers were in part, at least, contemporaneous. Paul's early
years spent at Tarsus and his concentration on interests related to pharisaic Judaism would account for his detachment from the work of Jesus during his active ministry.
More surprising is the limited number of quotations and
references to the tradition about the Master that was current among the members of the early Christian community.
Paul is acquainted with the basic content of this teaching,
but when it appears in his writings, it bears the stamp of
his own mind upon it. The main reason for this would
seem to be the special demand of a mentality like Paul's
in appropriating the meaning of the life and work of Jesus.
The appeal of the Galilean teacher would hardly come to
him in the same terms which impressed and elicited immediate response from the untutored fishermen and others
among the common folk who became Jesus' disciples. It
would be natural for the educated, earnest Pharisee to

think of these people more as a nuisance than the vanguard of a new day.

It is, therefore, not the historical Jesus who issues the main challenge to Paul. Although he refers to Jesus with reverence and affection, only the God of Israel or One enjoying a special relation to God defined by Judaism could command his total loyalty. In other words, as a devout and able man of faith, the terms of his acceptance of Jesus are already inwardly fixed. Those terms are set in the Jewish hope and thought concerning the coming Messiah. This fact presents the significance of the crisis on the road to Damascus. Whatever view one may take regarding the particulars of this experience, it was a genuine conversion in the literal sense of that word, and the core of it was Paul's recognition of the heavenly being who spoke to him that day as the Christ, the Anointed One, installed as Son of God by his resurrection from the dead.

The implications of this experience did not become clear all at once, but it was the starting point for a complete change of direction in Paul's life and thought. There is, in this thought, continuity with the historical Jesus through the early Christian community which had come into existence by virtue of the accomplishment of his mission, and which was to bear his name. But that name for Paul is to be Jesus *Christ,* the Lord, designating a role or function or office that transcends the work of the earthly Jesus and will complete it when he comes finally to establish his kingdom. It is from the Christ whom Paul knows by "revelation," whom he has resolved to know no more after the flesh, that

his gospel and vocation are derived. It is the conversion
experience that shatters the rigid Judaic mold, prepares the
way for reorganizing and refocusing the older elements of
his religion, and enables him to respond creatively to new
demands in the contemporary situation. This widening of
the horizons also opens the way for dedication to the Gentile mission in the hope of capturing for the elect of Christ
as many as possible before the End. It is to this task whose
urgency is marked by the shortness of the time and the personal need to excel in everything he does that Paul applies
himself without stint of energy or fear of sacrifice.

The resurrection of Jesus and the conversion of Paul are
two mutually related facts in the religious transformation
of the apostle. Although as Pharisee he held general views
about the resurrection, it is only by the conversion experience that he is able to penetrate to the deeper, more concrete understanding of it. He equates his vision on the road
with the witness of the disciples concerning the risen Lord.[1]
He has very special convictions about this revelation. It
came to him in a way unmatched by any of the other apostles. The inward subsidence of Saul, the Pharisee, struck
down in the very act of seeking more merit for righteousness before God under the law, is not unlike the opening
of the tomb and the deliverance of Jesus. Both are cata-
clysmic. What inwardly happened to the disciples by the
post-Calvary events also happened to Paul. The identification of Paul with Jesus, as Christ, is complete. He has been

---

[1] I Corinthians 15:3-11.

crucified with Christ, and it is no longer he that lives but Christ that lives in him, and the life he now lives, he lives by faith, not in Jesus but in the Son of God. Baptism has an eschatological significance.[2] It represents the end of the former life and the beginning of the new—an actual participation in the death and resurrection of Jesus by which he became the Christ of God, and Saul, the Pharisee, became Paul the apostle of the Christ. This is the relation of Paul to Jesus, and there can be no serious doubt about its genuineness.

It is by the meaning of the conversion experience that we understand also the extraordinary significance of grace in the teaching of Paul. Bent on a mission of destroying the Christians, convinced of his duty to carry out the mission with deadly intent, unwittingly flying in the face of God, blinded by fanatical zeal, the light shines and the voice speaks. At the moment of his most extreme opposition to the church when he was least deserving of favor, the truth dawns. While we were yet sinners, Christ died for us, and, without such death, this vision of him would not have been possible. It was something that happened outside the law when he was actually serving it; something in the realm of personal relations with God, transcending law, that makes faith in Christ the new way to God. It is the eschatological experience of Paul that enables him to see in new perspective the eschatology of Judaism. He was as one born out of his time; he was set apart for this work even before birth.

[2] Dodd, C. H., *The Epistle of Paul to the Romans*, pp. 92-93. New York: Harper & Brothers, 1932.

The "revelation" was the beginning of a new inner world whose foundations had to be rebuilt in a thoroughgoing intellectual reconstruction. In that task, Paul spent the remainder of his life.

The conversion experience also gives the clue to his mission to the Gentiles with whom he can now enter a relationship which he rejected as a boy in Tarsus where, as a member of a minority group, he felt separated and superior. This mission is his choice in the arrangement which he made with the pillar apostles whereby they should work among the Jews while he went to those outside Judaism. Such an understanding gave him a free field for the use of his powers and may have made for peace among the apostles. Once, Paul tells us, he withstood Peter to the face for improper conduct in applying the terms of the agreement on the matter of circumcision.[3] It is the work among the Gentiles that provides the occasion for rethinking his theological outlook as a Jew, but the deeper motive is the necessity of maintaining his own inner integrity in being obedient to the heavenly vision. He can know nothing that lies outside his experience of Christ crucified, though the preaching of that may be foolishness to those who hear without the support of this vivid conviction which is his unique possession.[4]

Another outstanding characteristic of Paul's theological reconstruction is the fact that it was worked out in the midst of the exacting daily routine of missionary and pas-

---

[3] Galatians 2:11-13.
[4] I Corinthians 2:2.

toral activities. He was in no sense an armchair thinker. What the product of that thinking was, in its more formal aspect, we may set down in briefest summary of the main issues, remembering the presuppositions we have already stated.

2. *The Gospel According to Paul*

What is the nature of the salvation offered in the gospel according to the great apostle? In a word, it consists of the removal of all barriers which stand between men and God. The first of these is bondage to spiritual powers other than God, including Satan and the evil spirits associated with him. To understand the importance of this, we need only recall the Jewish cosmology, or world view, of Paul's day.[5] It was a world inhabited by spiritual beings some of whom were beneficent agents of God in His dealings with men. Others were malevolent beings seducing men from noble purposes, interfering with their normal interests, entering into them and taking possession of their souls. As Paul sees it, Jesus, by his death and resurrection, has abolished the power of these evil spirits. His thinking on this point recalls the answer of Jesus to the scribes who charged him with being in league with Beelzebul. Jesus refutes the accusation by showing that a house could not be divided against itself and survive, and adds that the demons were subject to him because he used a power superior to that of

---

[5] A good, brief treatment of this subject will be found in S. Vernon McCasland's little book *By the Finger of God* (New York: The Macmillan Company, 1951).

their prince. As Jesus, during his earthly ministry, was master over evil spirits in their relations with men in particular cases, he is now, as a heavenly being, a complete master over their total domain. Men need no longer be subject to their intrusion. Christ has delivered them from this source of diversion from the purpose of God.

The second barrier which separates men from God is the condemnation under which they stand through transgression of the known will of God, both Jew and Gentile. In dealing with this problem, Paul's thought moves on the juridical plane. The state of man is somewhat like that of an accused person before a court of law, only in this case conviction of guilt is already a fact by virtue of man's actual condition.

Starting with this assumption, the first premise of Paul's reasoning is that man cannot of himself do anything to extricate himself from his dilemma. His second premise is that nothing short of acquittal will suffice. There is no middle ground. The terms of the law must be fully met and man does not have the capacity to earn acquittal by obedience to the law while any reliance on ritual observance is doomed to failure. The intensity of this conviction is rooted in Paul's acute sense of shortcoming in attaining a righteousness acceptable to God. His feeling in Romans is that the law, to which he was devoted, really played a trick on him. It offered him a standard to live by but no way of realizing the goal which it set, with the consequence of accentuating the extremity of his position. This, however, is true for all men. What then? The answer is that a "right-

eousness of God" has become available through Christ in
whom both God and man meet on grounds that satisfy the
demands of the revealed will of God in the law and this
makes acquittal possible. It was this which Christ accomplished by his death—justification. The third main premise
in Paul's thinking is that this provision for man's salvation
has been made on the initiative of God without reference
to anything that man deserves. This is the meaning of
grace. The fourth premise is faith, by which man may appropriate the gift of the new life in Christ. Thus men may
start all over again with release from the results of former
infractions of the law. There is "now," under these conditions, "no condemnation."

In the further thought of Paul, there is a deeper source
of estrangement from God closely bound up with his views
about the law. In this area, Paul discusses sin and its consequences in a dimension different from that involved in
his view of justification. Sin is a pervasive power in the
world, so real and active that Paul practically personalizes
it. It is universal and seeks dominion over men in both
their internal and external relationships. "All have sinned"
is a verdict that includes the Gentile because he has a revelation of God in the natural world and in his conscience.
He has failed to meet the standards of this revelation just
as the Jew has not met the demands of the revelation given
through Moses. Men are alienated, cut off from the life of
God, so that something more than a formal transaction is
necessary. Acquittal does not come to terms fully with
man's need. Sin involves more than legal guilt. It calls for

forgiveness, the closing of the gap between men and God in a personal sense that heals the broken relationship. The remedy for this is redemption and reconciliation. This is really the heart of Paul's gospel and emphasizes the need for personal transformation which he felt so keenly.

> God was in Christ reconciling the world unto himself. . . .
> . . . we pray you in Christ's stead, be ye reconciled to God.[6]

Again it is Christ's oneness with humanity and his unity with God that enables him to re-establish friendly relations and fellowship between men and God. In the death of Jesus the power of sin was destroyed by putting off the flesh that gave it opportunity while the resurrection attested his triumph over it.

All this came by "revelation" to Paul in the conversion experience and his subsequent examination of the issues which it precipitated. He came to understand that by his death, Christ disclosed a new insight into the character of God transcending the meaning of the law and inviting men to enter into relationship with him as a "new creation." Thus this act of God's grace, to which men may respond by faith, leads to deliverance from bondage to hostile spirits, sets aside the penalty of the law, and breaks the power of sin. Personal fellowship with God is restored and deepened, and moral union with Christ provides the condition for the working out of salvation in ethical goodness.

---

[6] II Corinthians 5:19, 20.

The foregoing, with many important aspects of Paul's theology left out, must suffice as we now turn to a more intimate inspection of his personal conflict as that took form in the development of his self-consciousness and his conception of his vocation.

3. *Thorn in the Flesh*

Turning to Paul's view of himself, we begin with his physical status. In examining the data connected with this issue, as well as those related to other questions, it is well to remember that Paul's language is often vivid and imaginative, struck off in the quick perception of the idea he is expounding, not to mention his employment of allegory as a canon of interpretation. With respect to his "affliction," it is impossible to say precisely what it was, although the fact of some continuing disability seems beyond reasonable doubt. His conception of the "flesh" is irrelevant here, for he did not think of the body as inherently evil but only the organ by which sin gets its hold on men. The intensity of Paul's wrestling with the problem, however, reflects his deep personal struggle to neutralize or rise above some severe and insurmountable limitation. On the hypothesis that the disorder was functional, it is worth noting that Paul had the sort of sensitivity which is commonly associated with neurotic tendency. There is some evidence that his ailment affected his eyes. In the account of the experience on the way to Damascus, it is said that he arose from the ground but could see nothing and had to be led by the hand into the city where he remained sightless for three days.

In the Galatian letter, he refers specifically to his bodily ailment and adds that the sympathies of the Galatians were so stirred that they would gladly have plucked out their eyes and given them to him.[7] This may be nothing more than the common figure of hyperbole to express the measure of their feeling toward him, but a more specific reference to his eyes is not ruled out if we take note of the statement at the end of the letter where he says, "See with what large letters I am writing with my own hand." It is a fact of observation that persons afflicted with hysterical blindness may show the symptom of very large handwriting. Whether we take this view or not of Paul's malady, it must be remembered that he was not continuously incapacitated by poor eyesight, for he worked regularly at his trade as a tentmaker which he could not have done had such an affliction been more than episodic. Hysteria, of course, would not necessarily involve organic deterioration of the eyes. This illustration is sufficient to show how inconclusive the evidence is for any specific illness that we can name in terms of modern diagnoses. Other views on this subject need not therefore detain us.

On the whole, it would seem more natural to conclude that Paul's physical deficiency, whatever it may have been in particular, resulted in a general reaction to his bodily appearance. There is evidence that he did not make a very

[7] Galatians 4:12-16.

favorable impression when he appeared in public. In Second Corinthians 10:10 (RSV), one of the notably autobiographical passages, he quotes an opponent who says that Paul's letters are "strong," but his "bodily presence" (literally, "appearance of his body") is weak, and "his speech of no account." The references of this sort add up to the general impression that Paul had some organic peculiarity or inferiority with emotional components which would produce earnest, compensatory striving. These compensations are illuminating as a part of the motivation of his extreme zeal in pursuing the religious goal he had set for himself in Judaism and in his later struggle for status and dominance in the churches.

Some of the evidence on the latter point is worth examining. Continuing the passage to which reference has just been made, Paul answers the opponent by saying, "Let such people understand that what we say by letter when absent, we do when present." He means that he will show his critics that he has the force equal to demonstration of power when personally present. There is sarcasm in the words, "Not that we venture to class or compare ourselves with some of those who commend themselves," and who measure themselves by "comparing themselves with one another." In contrast to this, Paul affirms that he judges himself by his own standards and when he boasts, he "boasts in the Lord." He keeps within the limits marked out by God, for only he whom the Lord recommends is accepted. It is probable that Paul would have found it difficult to utter these sentiments in public appearance before

the churches and his opponents at Corinth. He chides the
Corinthians for not saving him this trouble by coming forward and taking his part, and there is deep hurt in the
words, "I think that I am not in the least inferior to these
superlative apostles," and again, "Even if I am unskilled in
speaking, I am not in knowledge; in every way we have
made this plain to you in all things." [8]

The passage in Second Corinthians 11:16f is especially
revealing with respect to Paul's deeper feelings about himself in the presence of opposition. He says he is going to
play the fool for a moment to boast a little as worldly men
boast. Then he blurts out, "For you gladly bear with fools,
being wise yourselves!" He adds that they even pay the
fools who serve them "for you bear it if a man makes slaves
of you, or preys upon you, or takes advantage of you, or
puts on airs, or strikes you in the face. To my shame, I must
say, we were too weak for that!" After this, he lets go with
the details of his record that ought to silence even the most
blatant "fool." He is irked keenly because his opponent has
taken money from the church whereas he has never made
it his practice to accept any compensation. He has not been
a burden to anyone. He has supported himself by his trade.
He has asked only for gifts to minister to the needy saints
in Jerusalem. When he is through boasting, and feeling
badly about his defense of himself, he tells the Corinthians
that they "forced him to it." At the last, he refers to his
weakness and the glory of it, the thorn in the flesh which

---

[8] II Corinthians 11:1-6. (RSV)

becomes the source of the blessing of a sufficient grace. As the letter closes, he expresses the hope that they will not find him a failure, and accept this epistolary chastisement in lieu of a severity he would need to use in his projected visit to them. The critic had said that Paul acted humbly when he stood "face to face with you," but was "very bold" when he was away. It seems valid to conclude that Paul was quite timid in face-to-face relations, and that this was due, in part at least, to reaction to his own felt physical deficiency or peculiarity.

That Paul had strong feelings of hostility, these and other passages fully attest. In The Acts 9:1f, his attitude toward the Christians is described in terms of extreme violence. His own statement confirms this. Later the same fierce spirit is turned against those who are subverting his converts and those tendencies in his converts that imperil their loyalty to his gospel. He tells the Corinthians that anyone who does not love the Lord is to be "accursed," while the Galatians are warned that anyone who preaches a gospel contrary to his is also "accursed." He repeats this for emphasis. Using military language, he promises his critics that he will destroy their strongholds and "courtmartial" all who are guilty of insubordination. He will undermine the claim of those who are "deceitful workmen" and masquerade as apostles of Christ and "no wonder, for even Satan disguises himself as an angel of light." [9] Their end will be fitting for their deeds. Again in the early letter to the Corinthians, he

---

[9] II Corinthians 11:13-15. (RSV)

speaks of certain puffed-up individuals whom he will reduce to proper stature when he comes by giving a demonstration of power not confined to talk. He ends the discussion with the challenge, "What do you wish? Shall I come to you with a rod, or with love in a spirit of gentleness?" [10]

What do these words mean? The strong hand to hold the infant church to the mark? Yes. But they mean also that inwardly Paul knows his weakness. It is ever with him, the inescapable weight on his personality. Behind this hostility is a craving to be loved. It is perhaps the central characteristic of Paul's emotional character. To document this, we have only to note the passages where Paul beams with joy when anyone is deferential toward him. How he thanks God on every remembrance of the Philippians! How he mingles praise with denunciation on other occasions!

When a man feels he is unattractive; when a sense of inferiority weighs upon him; when isolation and loneliness threaten to cut him off from his fellows; then the craving for recognition and love becomes acute, and if this craving goes unsatisfied too long, hostility rises further to isolate the person, or, if expressed, uses the opposition aroused in others to justify the inner feeling of rejection. Fortunately for Paul, there was response to his efforts. Some people, notably Aquila and Priscilla, Timothy, Titus, Luke, the "beloved physician," and the long list of persons appended to the letter to the Romans gave Paul the honest regard which quieted this hot craving for response from others.

---

[10] I Corinthians 4:21. (RSV)

They bound up the wounds of isolation as well as tended his physical affliction. It is no accident that First Corinthians 13, the world's greatest panegyric on love, was written by a man who carried a load of hostility that threatened to shatter his soul. If, to all this, one wants to say, "Neurosis," the elements are there—feelings of rejection, compulsiveness, perfectionism, hostility, anxiety. But such a conclusion must face other facts.

4. *Sanity in Pastoral Care*

If the passages just cited were all the evidence that we have for understanding Paul's inward feeling about himself and his vocation, there would be reason for concluding that the motivation for his work was a neurotic drive for distinction. But such a judgment waits on an examination of Paul's behavior as an administrator and pastor in the presence of problems that created great difficulty in his churches. His striving for recognition, prestige, status above others, and his craving for love, must be set over against his actual performance in concrete situations which called for the most careful discrimination and decisive action. We turn next to some of the more important of these situations.

Considering the extreme paganism of the environment, probably no Christian leader ever faced a more complicated situation than that which occasioned the letters to the Corinthians. One among them had been guilty of extremely improper conduct—the "immorality" of a man "living with his father's wife." With this, Paul deals in no uncertain terms. The offender must be removed from the church, his flesh surrendered to destruction by Satan in order that his spirit may be saved. Then there is the matter of litigation. The Corinthian Christians in their disagreements are using secular courts of law to settle disputes among them. This ought not to be, for, in the true spirit of the love of Christ which they have received and the new role they are to have in the judgment of the world by virtue of their own justification, they ought to be able to adjust such matters as may arise among themselves. Surely, as those who are to be assigned to weighty matters in behalf of the whole world, they ought to be competent to manage these trivial things.

In the matter of eating food offered to idols, Paul shows none of the rigidity that might be inferred from some other passages. His thinking is very clear on the point, and his counsel is a logical outcome of the operation of a broad understanding in the spirit of love and brotherhood. Strict monotheist that he was, he says that for Christians, these idols do not exist at all as gods; what is done in service to them is therefore a mere empty form. It really does not matter whether one eats food of sacrifices to idols or not. It is not by eating or not eating that Christians commend themselves to God. There is, however, another consideration—the weaker brothers to whom the eating of the food may be a stumbling block. For their sake, and the good repute of the church, it is better not to eat such meat. The rule is: In whatever you do, make sure that it is to the glory of God and not offensive to Jews, to Greeks, or inimical to the church. If one is invited to dinner and one wants to go, let him eat whatever is set before him without raising any question on the ground of conscience. On the other hand, if the issue of food is raised in such a way as to compromise the Christian witness or damage anyone's faith, let one restrain himself in this matter. The sense of responsibility and prudence counsel this attitude.

Again, where will one find greater absence of dogmatism and more sound sense than in Paul's dealing with the question concerning speaking in tongues? The doctrine of the Spirit is central in Paul's gospel, but in the practical results of its acceptance among his converts it was susceptible to extreme applications that jeopardized wholesome living in the church. One could utter nonsense and say it was dictated by the Spirit. Paul treats the problem in the setting of his ruling principle of "diversities of gifts but the same Spirit." Not all have the same gift or the same function; indeed, this is to the advantage of the brotherhood since each profits by the special insight that comes from others. No rules are to be set up to control the ecstatic brother. He is, however, to be admonished about his failure to communicate a sensible message to the brethren if what he says is gibberish. It is better to say five words that edify than ten thousand that do not instruct. If therefore a communication cannot be interpreted to the advantage of others, let a man keep silent "in the church or speak to himself and to God," remembering that "God is not a god of confusion, but of peace."

Much has been written about Paul's famous discussion of sex and marriage in his Corinthian correspondence and of his own personal sexual adjustment. In its context, and the discriminating spirit which runs through all the passages, it is doubtful whether the mind of Paul expresses itself anywhere else with more sanity and balance. Here appears a characteristic of his outlook that is important in assessing his leadership. When he offers his views on a question of practical conduct, he says, "I say this of myself, not in the Lord." This makes the point that he considers himself subordinate to Christ, and that he also is deferring to what the spirit of Christ communicates to those who must make decision regarding the questions before them. Always, of course, his conviction assumes the imminence of the end of the age. Though many of his teachings about conduct have permanent value by virtue of their inherent ethical quality, this immediate application is for the limited period of waiting until Christ comes.

What is the upshot of his teaching about sex and marriage? Taking together all that he says, the following will summarize his position. *First,* there is no wholesale disvaluing of sex or any prudish attitude toward it in the thinking of Paul. *Second,* the relationship between husband and wife, as indeed all other relationships, partakes of a quality different from those outside the church by virtue of their being "in Christ"; that is, belonging to the new community which Christ is creating in his followers. Christians are people who have been transformed by faith in Christ. This is basic in Paul's answer, the key to all behavior of which he approves. *Third,* in the case of believers who are married to unbelievers, that fact should not be cause for divorce.

Indeed, there is advantage in their continuing together, for the believing one consecrates the unbelieving one, but there is no compulsion in this. If the unbelieving one desires to separate, let him do so, for we have been "called to peace." *Fourth*, with regard to the unmarried, it is his advice that they remain single, although Paul professes no "command from the Lord" on this. He gives his own opinion and leaves room for the working of the "Spirit of God." His reason is the present "distress"; "for the form of this world is passing away." What his word amounts to is a question of priorities. The Lord is coming. We wait for that event. Customary human relations are qualified by this fact. Present demands of our preparation for this event require that we be freed from anxieties of this present age, that our devotion to the Lord shall be wholehearted. Nevertheless, this may not be possible for all, especially for those whose "passions are strong." Hence, marriage is to be honorably accepted. *Fifth,* there is to be the utmost integrity in the personal behavior of the Christian. There is to be no posing or pretending. Paul's rule in all the churches is that "everyone is to lead the life the Lord has assigned to him." "Everyone should remain in the state in which he was called." Each is to be accepted by all on this basis.

Finally, as for Paul himself, marriage had to be given up deliberately. He says, "Do I not have the right to be accompanied by a wife as the other apostles and brothers of the Lord and Cephas?" Of course, he has the same right. It was the special demand of his apostleship, his life as itinerant missionary, the risks he had to take daily with death lurking along his way, to say nothing about the rigorous discipline of his vocation, that ruled out marriage for him. It was not a matter of neurotic compulsion, but a matter of practical decision in the presence of circumstances associated with his work. He speaks on this question with a high sense of responsibility as a Christian leader, and it may be added, parenthetically, that he shows a kind of permissiveness which even a modern counselor could respect. Indeed, it is remarkable, considering the premise of the *parousia,* that he did not take an authoritarian, absolutist position. Paul is deeply sensitive to the limitations of human nature and does not overload it. Rather he asserts that no temptation shall be greater than his converts can bear and that with the temptation, God will provide a way of escape from it.

But, for all his consideration of the individual Christian, Paul feels responsibility for the church as the living organism of Christ's presence in the world. The corporate life, the assembling together of the Corinthians must present unequivocal witness that they are in Christ and he in them. They have violated this principle in their celebration of the Lord's Supper. Divisions and favoritism, cliques and jealousies are appearing among them. These unhappy circumstances are robbing them of their spiritual integrity when they come to the Lord's table. "So then my brethren, when you come together to eat, wait for one another—if anyone is hungry, let him eat at home—lest you come together to be condemned." [11] Fellowship or community with

---

[11] I Corinthians 11:34. (RSV)

one another that is experienced in partaking of the Supper must not be corrupted by inequalities which surround their relations elsewhere, for if anyone partakes of the cup unworthily, that is, without discernment of its meaning, and has in himself attitudes that are destructive of joint participation with Christ in his suffering, he stands under a worse condemnation than that which the law assigned. "For by one Spirit we were all baptized into one body—Jews or Greeks, slaves or free—and all were made to drink of one Spirit." [12] In baptism there is a dying to the particular physical body that identifies one as Jew or Greek, and there is a rising of a body by the spirit like unto the resurrected body of the Lord. The body of the believer is no longer the body of his physical birth bearing the differentiating marks of race, for it has been quickened anew in Christ in whose image the believer is being progressively transformed. If anyone is in Christ, he is a new creation.

If, in addition to these further passages which describe Paul's sense of vocation, evidence of his personal balance is needed, one has only to look at the spirit of love which, despite his inward resentment, readily comes to the surface. He regrets that it was necessary to reprove the erring brother at Corinth, yet he rejoices that this action was the means of repentance and change. It was a "godly grief" he sought to induce, and he is glad that the church's own perception of the nature of the wrong and its attendant dangers confirmed his rebuke. And now he rejoices in the generosity

---

[12] I Corinthians 12:13. (RSV)

which he hopes will supply the proof of their unity with him and the other churches in their gifts for the saints in Jerusalem. Love is supreme among all virtues, even above faith and hope. Love which is active good will, the utter devotion to the positive doing of good to others is to be genuine, to be extended in the measure of outdoing one another in honor. It is this love, also, which transforms all human relations, even changing the character of a slave in the sight of his master—so "that he is no longer a slave but . . . a beloved brother."

By the evidence of all these attitudes, who will fail to see that the inward imbalance which may be observed in Paul was actually the source of creative genius looking for a cause worthy of its insight, its vision, and its energy? He came ultimately to his self-consciousness by identification with the Christ whom he adored. The limitations which he himself confessed were transcended by the vigor of spirit needed to fight the good fight, keep the faith, and bring many to salvation by his "gospel."

5. *Conclusion and Transition*

In adopting the concept of the "soul of Israel" for this part of our study, we have proceeded on an assumption which is common to all who look to the Scriptures for instruction and guidance. The diversity of situations disclosed in the Bible, presenting human behavior in forms ranging from its worst to its best, was seen to parallel the variety of experiences which, in some form, every man may recognize in himself, as he practices "the art and the theory of the internal life." Accepting the general idea of the "soul" which prevailed in Hebrew thought, we drew the main issue in terms of the struggle of the self to become person. We identified the tension between these two components of the inner life as the characteristic trait and condition of human self-consciousness and located the solution of the problem in the transmutation of the dynamics of the body-mind organism into communicable symbols. We saw the ebb and flow of this interaction in every situation where men of Israel wrestled with the stark realities of their times. Though manifest in the concrete occasions of both the early and the middle years, our most important insight came clearly to light in the work of the prophets where "the word of the Lord" and the vision of universal service, in detachment from national locale, presented the picture of believing man. Biblical man, in this character, formulating convictions which gave direction and drive to responsibility in the face of frustration, defeat, and despair, we recognized as the *person* living by faith. With this development, the adventure of Israel required only one transcendent event to establish ground and focus for the kind of belief that would shape man's further advance in religion. This was accomplished when "the Word became flesh" and the resurrection faith, first propagated by the disciples, transformed Saul, the Pharisee, into Paul, the Apostle. He, more than any other, led the way in founding a *believing community* for the nurturing of personhood in all men who would accept the work of God in Jesus Christ and thus encounter the ultimate nature of their own being and destiny.

The sum of the matter is that in Paul, the soul of Israel broke the bonds of the law and a rigidly set personality pattern, and reached out to fulfill the promise to Abraham that in him all the nations of the earth would be blest. His life was a supreme act of containment inwardly reconciling the claims of Judaism under challenge of the demands of personal salvation in the Graeco-Roman world. As Jesus achieved that intimacy of unity with the will of God which disclosed the meaning of real personhood, so Paul, transformed, spent himself in the effort to bring all peoples together in a community of universal love in order that the divine work in man might continue in subsequent ages.

As the calendar marks time, it is a long way from Jesus and Paul to the present century. The age in which they lived presents radical contrasts to ours. They seem remote from interests which daily engage our attention. Such a conclusion, however, when read too literally, fails to reckon with the ultimate fact of man's inward character and his capacity continuously to relive and reshape history. From this standpoint, biblical men are far from being alien to us. In spiritual kinship, they are closer than the neighbors next door. They touch us at the center of our being. They belong to internal events which are the substance of the soul and which make them partners with us in the adventure of personality. To make this fact real and authentic in religious living today will be our purpose in Part II of this work. We shall observe how meanings which flow from the

Bible may be translated into modern concepts of self-consciousness, recapitulation and transcendence, crisis and redemptive grace; how man, the person, clothed in the gar-
ment of modern culture, is at heart the same sort of being
as his earlier brother who walked in Palestine twenty centuries ago; and how, through all changes of temporal settings, God's act in Jesus Christ continues to work with
power at the center of man's need for salvation.

PART II   *Man the Person*

6. BIOLOGY AND CULTURE

1. *Biblical Man and Biology*

AMONG THE INSIGHTS WHICH EMERGE from our study of the soul of Israel, none is more outstanding than the fact that man, as we saw him there, thought of himself in separation from nature. This is the main feature of his self-consciousness and it expresses itself in the view that he bears a special relationship to God, his Creator. This conviction appears on the first pages of Genesis. It is perpetuated and elaborated in the idea of the covenant, the concept of the chosen people, and the visions of world mission in the Second Isaiah. Only Job and Ecclesiastes seriously question it. It is rebaptized in the Gospels and Epistles and ends with a shout of triumph in Revelation. In this fact, as in no other, the source of tension between the biblical view of man and the scientific view is to be found. The consequences for the internal life we must now examine.

With respect to the attitude of the Hebrews toward nature we have already noted two facts. Like all other human beings, in all times, they used the resources of nature to sustain life and to advance the interests of security. They also had a strong sense for order. They differentiated objects and processes from one another. The priestly mind was especially occupied with this kind of thinking. With meticulous care, to the point of tedium, it was constantly drawing lines, fixing boundaries, for the purpose of keeping a people holy, acceptable unto the Lord. This also is the interest of law and moral idealism distinguishing between right acts and wrong ones, and to this extent separating parts of man's life from other parts. To place things and keep them where they belong on the basis of common agreement is to be sure of them and to control them.

Of special importance is the biblical view concerning animals. They are created by God. They have in them the breath of life. They exist for man who names them and thereby puts them in their place. In the Holiness Code found in Leviticus 17-26, most careful attention is given to distinctions between the "holy and the common," the "clean and the unclean." There are dietary laws governing what shall be eaten and what is taboo. The Hebrew writers show extensive knowledge of animals observing their characteristics and classifying them. The underlying motive is religious and expresses the desire for definiteness and aversion to mingling things which do not belong together. Everything, "after its kind," is to be kept in the state fixed by its origin.

Aside from his connection with them in a common Creator and the use of some of them for food and beasts of burden, biblical man has only one other purpose for animals. The best of certain species are selected for sacrifice to God in expiation of guilt and atonement for sin. But one thing biblical man never does is to make explicit acknowledgment of his likeness to the animals, that biologically the processes in him have their counterparts in them. The reason is obvious. He is not analytic. He takes a gross view of the body. He notes its visible members and names them. In preparing animals for sacrifice, he sees the similarity of their internal organs to those of his own that incidentally, on occasion, come into view. Blood is especially important. It is equivalent to life. But he knows nothing about its circulation and its specific properties or functions. He experiences pain but does not describe it with awareness of the existence of nerves. He has no word for brain. He cherishes fertility and reproduces his kind like the mammals associated with him. He experiences deep emotions. He knows euphoria, what it means to suffer, and has organic reactions of sympathy. The word translated "compassion" in the New Testament has a strong visceral connotation. For all his lack of exact knowledge about anatomy and physiological functioning, it must be set down as essential fact that the true Israelite has respect for the body. It is "good" like everything else that God made. Even Paul returns to this in his reconstruction of faith. The ruling idea, however, is that man is made in the image of God, a "little lower than the angels." In this, the Hebrew affirms his self-acceptance.

In the light of the account just given, it seems odd that biblical ideas about the body, essentially wholesome, should

have suffered distortion in the setting of the scientific en-
lightenment of modern times. Yet this is what happened.
The sincere and eloquent statesman, William Jennings
Bryan, brought a career of frustration to an end by undertaking a rear-guard action against evolution. Many good
people looked upon him as their champion and would still
vote for him on that count. Some found entertainment in
the amusing scenes of the Scopes trial at Dayton, Tennessee,
where Clarence Darrow was trying to deface the image of
God. Other people were indifferent to the shadowboxing
that went on there. The affair, however, is a good example
of the resistance which human beings will offer to questions
that penetrate their defenses against a too realistic exposure
of facts about themselves. This trait is so characteristic of
human nature that it needs always to be considered in seeking to open minds which have been closed by error and
prejudice. The terms on which men accept themselves are
reflected in their ego-image where the guard is usually up.

2. *Man a Part of Nature*

We call the crusade of Mr. Bryan a "rear-guard" action because long before 1920, science had begun to introduce a
new era of human good by using the new knowledge concerning man's relation to nature, especially to other animals.
In fact, it was just about 250 years ago that Jean Fernel
and his immediate successors started a line of inquiry which
set important questions in a perspective destined to produce
better answers. The results of proceeding upon the assump-

tion that man is a part of nature have been so far-reaching and beneficial that it would seem impossible any longer to doubt the fact. The advance of modern medicine in the cure and prevention of disease has been made possible because the lower animals have the same basic biology as man and therefore can be used in the search for lifesaving measures. Today anyone who calls a doctor subscribes to the doctrine of man's kinship with the animals whether he believes it or not. A recent and most heartening example of this fact is the success of the Salk vaccine in immunizing children against poliomyelitis. When we pay tribute to the scientists who collaborated in this discovery we should not forget our "little brothers," to use the language of St. Francis, among the animals who made their bodies laboratories for the experimentation and testing whose results will increasingly guarantee security against this plague to millions of children.

Once the break is made and the mind is open to the facts, it does not take long for an intelligent person to see that when all the evidence is in, the special attributes of man are as intact as they ever were. Indeed, letting in the light to dispel superstition and prejudice gives more solid ground for human dignity and worth and a sense of belonging in the universe which, in another way, was the motivation of Hebrew thought. As the end-result of an age-old process in which many complicated steps and hurdles were negotiated, man looks better to himself, for he can gain some understanding of what it cost to produce him.

Yet man does not stand apart from all he has been. His

past is still in him as his future is before him. He appears
in direct continuity with one of the first stages of primordial life—the cell. The cell is the basic unit of every living
thing. No doubt important events preceded its emergence,
but once it was established as a unit of creation, the way
was open for everything that was to come. What a living
cell is, anybody can see by taking a drop of water from a
pool and putting it under a microscope. The two main
characteristics of this one-celled animal are to be found
wherever there is life. It maintains itself as an individual.
It has a boundary or membrane that encloses a nucleus and
the cytoplasm. It sustains itself by osmosis or by engulfing
food particles. Its other concern is to reproduce itself. It
does this by splitting in two, an event called fission. All this
goes on indefinitely. The law of the cell seems to consist
solely in keeping alive and multiplying its kind.

Though the cell always remains individual it will, under
certain conditions, associate itself in a symbiotic relationship with other types of cells and live a joint or corporate
life. The achievement of this kind of community had enormous consequences for the development of higher, more
complex forms or organisms culminating in man. At birth
the human infant has 15,000 million individual cells. By
the time adulthood is reached, it will have 1,000 billion,
about 12 billions of which will be in the brain.[1] Each body

---

[1] Sherrington, Sir Charles, *Man on His Nature,* pp. 94, 104. New
York: The Macmillan Company, 1941.

Herrick, C. J., *Brains of Rats and Men,* p. 4. Chicago: University of
Chicago Press, 1926.

cell continues its own existence as an individual, but one of the conditions of its union with other cells is the guarantee of food supply. To accomplish this, nature developed a division of labor whereby certain groups of cells, such as those which the lungs comprise, would serve the entire community in the function of supplying oxygen, the fuel required by the total energy system. The cells of the heart and the blood co-operate in this enterprise.

Food is likewise processed by progressive conversion into chemical units which can be carried to all the cells by the blood. Every schoolchild is asked at some time to trace the course of a bite of food and report on what happens at each stage of the journey from mouth to the ultimate consumer in body tissue. The "smoke" from the burning of food is returned to the lungs to be exhaled as carbon dioxide, and other unused or waste matter finds its way out of the body through the organs of excretion. All this, with much more, adds up to the basic fact that the survival and functioning of the individual cells require this sort of operation by which external environment—air, water, and all that goes under the collective term "food"—is mediated to them. In short, the body is a factory of continuous chemical activity of a very refined and efficient form.

In this very abbreviated picture of the body as an organism consisting of cells and specialized organs maintaining their individual existence and also working together, the timing of operations is a crucial matter. Provision is made for this in the central nervous system and its auxiliary divisions. This system is composed of cell units called neurons.

They are laid end to end, so to speak, for the purpose of establishing connections among all parts of the body. The system is a vast network of fibers through which, by electrical transmission, impulses continually unify the organism so that it can act effectively as a whole. It is a genuine case of one for all and all for one.

The sensory nerves in contact with the outer environment convey stimuli to the centers of reaction, interpretation or transmission, whether in the brain or spinal cord, to effectuate adjustments which will serve the needs of the organism at a given time and in such manner that it will act for the best interests of the individual. These reactions may be short-circuited by a facilitation which is a summation of previous learning processes. This enables the individual to make rapid responses in an unconscious manner without the necessity for stimuli to go to the center of interpretation in the brain and to return to the effector organ.

As the body gains experience in contact with environment these processes become conditioned in ways that affect later responses. Pavlov's dog, for example, after a series of feedings associated with the ringing of a bell, salivated when the bell only was used as stimulus. If we extend the point of this illustration to the limits of the situations which confront the individual human being we gain a fair idea of the range of his capacity to relate himself to environment. If we add to the involuntary reactions of the organism those which proceed from conscious thought given to the solution of problems, the total picture of the complication and effectiveness of the body discloses the supreme masterpiece of nature's art. If at this point we ask, What is all this for? and look for the answer in the history of the organism itself, we find that it is the same for man as it is for the cell—to survive as individual and to reproduce. Whatever else may be said about human nature, this must be said first. What may be said at last remains to be seen, but even now we harbor the conviction that nature's activity in man as in all other creatures that have preceded him, and surround him, is directed toward the accomplishment of the ultimate of possibility for him.

Man is the child of earth's old age. In him, the essentials of the entire evolutionary process selectively adjusted to time relations are recapitulated. The advanced step in this case appears in the extraordinary development of the outer layer of the brain variously called the cerebral cortex, neopallium, and the roof-brain. This structure composed of cells in contact with one another is the organ of mind, not in the sense that mind is localized in it, but in the sense that mind as a phenomenon appears in association with it, and, apart from it, no mind is known in nature. The exact relationship between mind and the brain remains an unsolved riddle. What we know about mind is derived mainly by inference from behavior of animals and man. This behavior always involves the body and the brain. The intimacy of mind with brain is disclosed by changes in mental activity induced by injury to the brain cells, drugs, and surgery. It cannot be said that mind is energy in a strict physical or chemical sense, but there is no question about its capacity definitely to effect action upon environment.

Thoughts are said to have "force," but that is a statement
which has meaning only in a setting other than that provided by the brain. For instance, scientific examination of
the brain of Albert Einstein may not be expected to yield
the mathematical equations of the Theory of Relativity.
Another feature of mind is the fact that it is always individual and has a history that can be examined by nonchemical
techniques. In terms of its relation to the behavior of the
organism, one clear and decisive fact that science discloses
about the function of mind is what Sherrington has described as the capacity to narrow the motor act from a general (abstract) purpose to a "specific purpose fitting a specific (concrete) occasion." [2]

An important conclusion emerges at this point. The human organism is a body-mind organism, not a body and a
mind, but a unified system of closely knit relationships designed to function always as a whole. An example will
enable us to visualize this general observation.

Imagine a man in a machine shop working at a lathe. He
is *standing*. In that position, we have the functioning of
bone structure, the skeleton holding him erect, muscles
supporting that structure, all of the delicate mechanism
within the brain and spinal cord maintaining equilibration
and keeping him balanced before his task. His *hand* guides
the piece of steel which he is shaping under the watchful
eye that keeps contact with the machine and the blueprint
at his side. *Heart, lungs,* and *other circulatory organs* are

---

[2] Sherrington, *op. cit.*, p. 233.

doing their work (all unnoticed) of supplying energy to the various organs (made up of individual cells) which are serving the ends of the man in his work. We have here a single complicated co-ordination of many functions concentrating upon each step of the task. The man's *mind* is the spearhead of the operation, but he is supported by all his biological equipment in accomplishing the one thing in view. Elaboration of this abbreviated description will reveal in terms of successive types of activity the human organism as it is in its behaving, ranging over the entire human scene whether preparing a field for cultivation, building a house, preparing a meal, driving a car on a busy street, writing an essay, or sitting in church on Sunday morning. There are, of course, varying degrees in which the organism is activated. On occasion there may appear to be outward passivity, but there is no lack of evidence that the body-mind combination is constantly functioning. Only in normal sleep or sedation or some other induced interruption is the mind disengaged from attention to some performance through bodily activity.

The illustration makes clear one of the distinctive features of human nature, the unique means by which the body maintains its unity in its operation upon environment. Without the central nervous system, the most noteworthy part of which is the most recent in the evolutionary scale—roof-brain or cortical sheath of the cerebrum—engaging the subordinate segments extending down the spinal column and completing the autonomic system, our man at the lathe would be inconceivable. Focal control, commanding the body as a whole through the co-operation of various centers in brain and cord and serving the end outlined in the blueprint, is the main fact.

This is the picture of the human organism shaping the physical environment. This is man in the role of creator—taking his world in hand by mind and making it over to suit his desires and purposes. The story need not be pursued further at this point, for common observation presents to everyone sufficient detail to round out what is here suggested. Suffice it to say that modern man continues to behave in accord with an injunction perceived by his ancient predecessor whose conquests warranted his belief in his power to subdue the earth. He could affirm that without knowing the nature of the body-mind organism that was himself; without, for all his wondering, even asking the questions which science has pursued relentlessly with extraordinary precision and result. The ancient intuition survives in the repeated and expanded operations of human history, and the end is not yet.

3. *Culture and Control*

In our description of the man above, we used certain words which took for granted an enormous development in human activity. We spoke of a "machine shop," a "lathe," a piece of "steel," and a "blueprint." What are these things? Everybody knows, but what do they tell us about man? Implicit in them is the whole story of what we call civilization or culture using the terms in their broadest sense. They stand for the work of man in converting objects, physical nature, into forms more congenial to the purpose of his adventure on this planet. The lathe is a tool, complicated, power run, descendant of a stone shaped to dig, to grind, or to cut. The modern combine in the farmer's field is the successor of the flint sickle and the flail. The ancient wheel has its progeny in the automobile and your wrist watch. Our lathe is the symbol of how far man has come in modifying environment by the invention of better tools and the use of power other than that available in animal muscles. The story of this development reaches back into the distant past. The age of steel, however, is a far cry from ancient metal-working in the manner of its refinement from crude ore and the multiplicity of its uses. Time would fail to tell about plastics made from vegetation; clothes that never had contact with sheep; butter produced without cows; and machines with electronic "brains."

Culture includes also those activities and arrangements which man has developed as a result of his mastery over nature. In gross effect, culture is the environment which man has made for himself, the social outcomes of the work of his hands directed by the roof-brain and its correlate mind. The blueprint in our illustration has a history that goes back to the drawings of prehistoric man on the walls of the cave in which he lived. The capacity to express observation in symbol, to translate objects and acts into grunts and then into polysyllables, to utter thoughts in pictures and meanings, has been among the achievements of great consequence in human development. The fertility of abstract idea, uniting a clue here with a clue there, conjuring up possibilities beyond anything early man dreamed, has incited all sorts of adventure ever unfolding into unprecedented transformations of nature.

The time has come when the unbelievable is the event to be expected. Our own world is replete with objects that have their counterparts in former times, but so far transcended in variety and utility as to make ours an entirely different world. The conviction grows that only the unimaginable lies outside the range of possibility. Given time, some new tools and adequate power, man may yet make the journey to the moon and survive the experience long enough to report his discoveries there, mayhap to reside there for a season. Indeed, is it beyond possibility to imagine that the earth, surrounded by her sister planets, may be the cradle for nurturing the kind of beings who will one day migrate by progressive stages to inhabit some of them and develop the resources for a kind of existence that would be as far from man as amoeba now is from the man we know? To use a figure, could it be that earth may turn out to be a laboratory of the universe for conducting an experiment that will affect the destiny of other planets? If and when such should be the case, the roof-brain or its successor will show the way. Meanwhile, as we said, the down-to-earth fact seems to be that nature's tendency to play out to the end the utmost of possibility for all her creatures is well on its way in man.

On the heels of this comes another thought. A foul regression or the end may be nearer than we think. It may be that man may play himself out before the day of his ultimate chance comes. The roof-brain still has its problems. It has done remarkably well. Taking the old animal body, rejecting specialized adaptation for a generalized one, it has shown amazing resourcefulness in inventing new combinations that extend the power of that body to extraordinary limits. The chief problem is the one man has always wrestled with—the problem of control, of direction of the energies which he has released. If the past is a guide, this problem will not be solved by repression, but by creative advance in a continuing adventure of exploiting available and unused opportunities.

The most intriguing and exciting fact about the history of living things, especially man, is their zest to fulfill themselves by evolving new adaptations which, acting reflexively on the creature itself, change it. Time is putting the pressure on; speed, the rate of change, is accelerating and laying on mind a burden of adjustment and responsibility it has never known before. The current age is rich beyond measure in its productivity. It is also wasteful in almost the same degree. Nature has always been extravagant as though relying on inexhaustible resources. Fossils and artifacts attest this. The huge experiment of the massive dinosaur with a brain excessively small in relation to body size, to mention only one act of prodigality, is an example. Civilizations of man himself have come and gone. But, for the nonce, he remains apparently in stronger stride than ever. How much of the world and of himself can he waste and keep a margin of safety against extinction? That is the question. What will he do about himself? No other creature can ask such a question. That it can be asked offers hope.

As a matter of fact, man has given much attention to the control of himself and has established the means of it. The provisions for this are a part of his culture. They take the form of folkways, customs, and institutions. The predominance of any of these means of control expresses, in general, the stage of a civilization and the measure of the forces that demand regulation. All these means arise from the demands of social living which intensify man's feeling and concern about himself. In large or complex societies, the chief form of control is institutional although custom, dictating distinctions of right and wrong, continues to play an important part. Institutions are arrangements for patterning behavior of individuals. For a long time in world history, five have persisted and continue to do duty—the family, the state, industry, the school, and the church or its counterpart. A sixth should be added—the professional arts, as distinguished from the fine arts. Each of these is a complex of human behavior of wide variation, and is also the patterning of that behavior within them. Like all things human, they are basically dynamic. In thinking of them, it is, therefore, useful to view them as uniform ways by which a society conserves and promotes its multiple interests in an orderly fashion that will guarantee its survival in the face of internal and external threat. Thus institutional arrangements reflect the basic orientation of the human organism.

Any attentive reading of human history will disclose the

fact that man has never been able to establish institutions that were completely adequate as agents of control at a given time or that attained permanence in any particular form. The reason for this seems twofold. First, the variations in individual behavior offer resistance to organization that would too closely confine them. This is related to a second and more fundamental fact, already hinted at, that man individually and collectively is an energy system constantly expressing himself dynamically and inducing changes that cannot be quickly incorporated into a given system of control. Institutions, precisely for the reason that they are regulative, tend to become set. But life, being dynamic, expressing fertility for acting in new combinations of ways, tends to move out from under institutions. The banks of a river normally keep the water within bounds until there is a change in the volume and force of the stream. Then the countryside is inundated to a point determined by more adequate barriers.

Control has taken many forms in the past and continues to be the issue in every decision. Early man recognized the necessity of marking out certain limits beyond which it was unsafe for him to go. He learned this from experience. As he became more sophisticated, liberated from some of his early fears, he sought to develop general techniques for defending himself against physical forces which threatened him. He divided nature into two categories on the basis of what served him and what harmed him. He thought that the world was permeated by a diffused impersonal power which he called *mana*. This power could support his efforts provided he made the right approach to it. If he made a mistake, such as Uzzah with good impulse made when he sought to shore up the ark on the way from Beth-shemesh, or by some deliberate action got out of bounds, he ran risks of becoming a victim of *mana*. In time this impersonal power was invested in personal beings or gods who had their abodes in certain designated places such as Mount Olympus among the Greeks. These beings were endowed with traits that were quite human in many ways, but it was important that men should keep in their good graces and not overstep the boundaries. Prometheus was chained to his rock because he stole fire from the gods and brought it down to men. We should not smile at this way of thinking and behaving, for we have among ourselves the same tendencies in our institutions and customs. We are even regulated by what we call etiquette, by whose rules we seek to do the right thing at the right time in our social relations. Specialism also has given rise to another whole system of regulation. People become expert in something. They occupy a certain place in society by virtue of their attainment, perhaps enjoy the prestige of a profession. They set bounds for themselves, resist encroachment, and others limit their action by avoiding the transgression of breaking over into a field forbidden by the taboos of specialism.

All this is sufficient to make the point that the more complex a society becomes, the more the regulative tendency emerges for the purpose of keeping everyone in his place. As these new ways of behaving become established, institutions are revised to define and limit them. They are given formal sanction by legislation whose production line in our capitals is constantly at work. In a hundred years, crime has increased 400 per cent, not because men are worse now than they were then, but because new laws responding to social change have multiplied the ways of getting out of bounds. On the international scene, we are now wondering how to keep atomic energy in a safe place. Something must be done to prevent this new Promethean fire from destroying the human race. This means, in effect, that in a society like ours, the human being must learn to adapt himself to the changes that are constantly going on. The rate of change is accelerated with a resulting burden and threat to the human organism that can be met only by continual institutional reconstruction and increasing measures to prevent breakdown. Is the human mind adequate for this task which involves the saving of itself as a phenomenon peculiar to man? Something tells us that it has not yet played itself out.

The process for meeting this situation takes us back to the meaning of the blueprint in our illustration. The existence of this piece of paper with lines and figures on it expresses one of the central sources of man's ability to adapt himself to environment at any time and to institute new change. This development stems from the invention of the capacity for speech or communication. It would seem indeed that when man acquired this ability, he added immeasurably to his power to solve his problems, for by it he was able to mobilize the thinking of others of his kind, to create situations with mutual stimulation, to tap the resources of many observers, to exchange insights and judgments and plan co-operative actions which offered the best promise of success. More than that, much more, through conserving experience by symbolic (verbal) record, knowledge was funded providing starting points for successive generations with an accumulative advantage for further advance.

Thus speech, as a highly co-ordinated operation within the brain, utilizing special portions of the body, became the agent of mind *par excellence,* facilitating inward manipulation of the external world in solving problems in the abstract before executing the appropriate external responses. How nature took the larynx, the palate, the tongue, and the lips of the animal head and co-ordinated them in skillful use of air from the lungs to issue in speech as the means of externalizing the productions of mind, is a story rivaled only by counterparts in eye and ear. The ear, originally adapted to provide defense against danger, and the guttural sound to frighten enemies or coax a mate, advances in man to an arrangement whereby he can hear himself think while he talks to his kind. The multiple contact of the mind with the outer world is thus balanced by multiple responses of sound-evoking symbols which may be allowed to dissipate in the air or by the hand, or other means, be set down in a permanent record. Communication is the epitome of mind, the ultimate stuff of its operation, and the continuous mode of its development.

4. *The Self*

One more topic must be mentioned in the context of mind and culture. That is the emergence of the self. Psychologists have adopted various methods in attempting to give a genetic account or explanation of how the human organism becomes a self. At this point, we shall remain in the stream of thought we have been following, leaving for discussion elsewhere a more adequate treatment to which the account here is introductory.

The term self is reserved for human beings. This does not mean that animals fall outside the category of highly integrated organisms that act as wholes in environment. Those which man has domesticated and which live out their existence in close association with him seem to approximate patterns of behavior that look human. To attribute self to them, however, is an unwarranted anthropism. The projection of our feelings toward them expresses only their usefulness to us or our care of them as creatures dependent upon us. The conditions for the emergence of the self have already been described—the arrival of the great brain of man whose resulting activity in human association developed a culture which expanded and intensified his experience as a living creature. We have observed also the tendency of mind to operate in terms of integrated wholes made up of parts and bearing an individual configuration. The most important whole for the human individual is another human individual perceived in the gross bodily form with alertness to penetrate and appropriate the inner quality, attitude, and feeling of the other.

It is the presence of other bodies and selves in communication with the child that nurtures his awareness of himself. Other selves have their own being differentiated by inescapable marks. They react and interact. They express likenesses and unlikenesses. They are individual. Roles or characteristic behavior, disclosed by words and actions, moods and manner, present a kind of integrated mode of behavior, not always consistent, but always associated with a particular body, gesture, and voice. It is observed also that these roles overlap at times. They may exchange functions. To a certain extent, father can be like mother, but their respective acts are never separable from the whole which each presents.

It is in this setting that the child becomes a self. He identifies himself with one then the other. He adopts selectively their attitudes, their feelings, their words, but they turn out in the end to be his, for his integration of them is individual, marked by variations and discoveries that belong to him and to no other. The variations may become exciting incentives toward elaboration. If checked by the necessities of social living, the urge continues in another direction, aided always by the concurrent development of brain and mind. The direction coerced may itself open up new avenues of adventure. Inhibited at one point, action finds another route that combines with still others, playing itself out over the whole range of possibility presented by each successive situation. Besides the parents are other children and adults who enlarge the field of experience. Ties are strongest with those who are nearest and with whom one most constantly lives, but the new self is really something new under the sun. Acts and feelings are conserved, stored, so to speak, as the fund for being human and the marks by which one knows he is a self in roles that preserve continuity with his social past and provide stability for future exploration.

In short, the self, with the aid of mind, organizes into unity the diversities of the external world of nature and of men. It recapitulates past experiences in the presence of new situations and reacts to them in the terms set by its own perception and meaning. This form of adaptation is made possible by the capacity to use verbal symbols which inwardly indicate to the self what the response should be and provide means for communicating that response to others. This communication is an act that expresses the transcendence of self and, with increasing mastery of language, vastly extends the range and quality of human living. It is thus that body, mind, and culture collaborate in laying the foundation for the transformation of a self into a person. The latter process, as we shall see, is at the center of the religious adventure of mankind.

7. THE PROBLEM OF MAN

THE EARLY GREEKS AND THEIR ASSOCIATES, the Phoenicians, living in a land of broken coastline and surrounded by islands, were among the first to experiment with water transportation.[1] In the sixth century B.C., they had in use, mainly for purposes of war, a ship called the galley. Some of these craft were a hundred and fifty feet long and twelve feet wide. The shell was crescent-shaped with a towering prow and a stern, sometimes ornamented like the head and the tail of a dragon. The chief feature of this vessel was the provision for increasing the power needed to navigate such bulk and weight. It was equipped with mast and sail for using the wind, but more characteristic was a system of propulsion by man power. The larger ships were of two types, the bireme with two banks of oars, and the trireme with three banks on each side. Each oar was operated by a man,

---

[1] Paul Herrmann, German scholar and editor, in his book *Conquest by Man*, p. 61, published by Harper & Brothers, 1954, states that the Egyptians developed watercraft thousands of years before the Christian era and had sea transportation at least *by the second half* of the fourth millennium B.C.

and the total number in the crew sometimes reached a figure of one hundred or more requiring space of as many
feet of the total length of the ship. Captives taken in war
were sentenced to duty as galley slaves and were chained to
their posts. Their activity was co-ordinated by an alert
taskmaster under the direction of a captain on the upper
deck. The chamber in which the oarsmen were stationed,
just above the water level, was called the *thalamus*. Later
the term came to mean any kind of secret or hidden
chamber.

1. *The Frontier of Mind*

The point of the story just reported subsists in the fact that
in the human midbrain, lying at the base of the cortical
region, there is a mass of nerve fibers which bears the name
thalamus. This is known to be the evolutionary survival of
the so-called "endbrain" of the reptiles of the Jurassic period.[2] Its position and general function in the human brain,
associated with another nerve center called the hypothala-
mus, parallels the account of the galley ship above. In that
description, certain words were used that can be translated
into the more refined terminology of anatomy. The thalamus of the galley is the source of *power*. The thalamites are
chained, organized into the total system by which the boat
is operated in navigation and directed by the *authority* of
the upper deck which fronts out upon environment and
adapts the course of the ship as a whole to each successive

[2] Berry, R. J. A., *Your Brain and Its Story*, p. 10. London: Oxford
University Press, 1939.

situation involved in the journey from one port to another.

Similarly, the thalamus and the cerebral cortex, or roof-brain, and their connections with the autonomic centers, become the means by which human life is run. The roof-brain discriminates events of the external world and responds with direction. The thalamic system mediates the energies that occasion requires. At birth, the thalamus is well developed, but the roof-brain is hardly more than a pulpy substance with elementary differentiation having, however, vast potentiality. The roof-brain grows under social stimulation, and its main problem is to transform animal instinctual energy released through the thalamus and so to organize that energy that the resulting life will be that of a human being instead of that of a mere animal. The thalamus when it was the "endbrain" of the saurian animal was in the place of power to release reaction to external demand with direct and effective result. In the more advanced state, the potential in this energy, currented through the refinements of the roof-brain, fires the motives of man's larger, more inclusive and complicated purposes. The thalamus has important bearing upon basic emotions which continue to be useful to human action although later developments in the brain have progressively superseded the older function until, in fact, "even symbols suffice as stimuli for the gratification and release of instinctual tensions.[3]

[3] Grinker, Roy R. in *Studies in Psychosomatic Medicine—an Approach to the Cause and Treatment of Vegetative Disturbances* edited by Franz Alexander and Thomas Morton French, p. 47. New York: The Ronald Press Company, 1948. Used by permission.

This reference to the thalamus and its connection with our animal history presents to us a scene where, acknowledging that we are a part of nature and in continuity with all events that have gone before, we must apply ourselves again and again to get our bearings with respect to the nature of the human adventure. The search for understanding ourselves goes unceasingly on. The reconstruction that science, with painstaking care, has now achieved in setting before us the essential facts about the course of events on this planet, is inviting and sobering. It stirs us because it is our own story. The "characters" that move across the stage in successive ages of earth-time, with their descendants continuing their role in the present, are a part of the unfolding drama in which we as man emerged very late, not more than a half million years ago.

Could we bring together in one grand assemblage living representatives of every form of life that is known to have existed, ranging from the one-celled paramoecium to the multicellular mammal that is ourselves, what a scene it would make! If we arranged them in the settings of their times, what engaging panorama of climatic shifts amid the lights and shadows of geological time would appear! If we saw them behaving in character, we would be fascinated by the exquisite beauty and variegated form of some of the creatures, their solitariness, their teaming up according to their kind, their playfulness, their cunning, their prowess. If our view extended to mealtime, the scene would suddenly change into a terrifying dream. The quieter herbivora would satisfy their hunger by foraging among the plants, but the carnivora would leap at the throats of their neighbors. Before our eyes, the whole earth would seethe with violence and, when the meal was over, the after-dinner scene would present a mangled disarray of leftovers and the sleep of the living with a full stomach among the dead. At the next meal, there would be fewer of some species and, if they happened to be less able to defend themselves, it would be easy to predict their extinction unless, by strength or cleverness, they could do better next time.

If then making as close inspection as we could, we took a final look and sought to generalize all the behavior we saw, what would we say? What we have said before with one addition. First, every living creature is bent on keeping itself alive as an individual. Second, every living thing is bent on keeping itself alive as a species by reproducing itself. Third, aside from inorganic elements directly taken from nature, all life is maintained at the expense of other life. Every plant and animal is a chemical factory that may serve the chemistry of another that feeds off it. Any revulsion that we may feel toward the aggregation of creatures we have envisaged and any thought that we are related to them would be followed by the admission that in all three of these respects, we are indeed like them. With these three concerns and their ramifications, we, man, occupy our time. Man recapitulates in himself all these activities, but with radical differences that are his distinguishing marks.

2. *Conflict and the Self*

Nevertheless, as far as observation, research, and imagination can lead us, conflict has been a continuous feature of affairs connected with the operations of nature and remains conspicuously at the center of human biology, human mentality, and human society. It is by opposition of forces in the curvature of space that the planets and the stars hold to their orbits with remarkable freedom from collision. It is by muscle fibers set against one another that energy enables the body to act upon objects in the environment. It is by problem situations that reason is aroused and new meanings created. It is by inward division that personality is shattered and made useless and dangerous in social relations. It is by strife between interests of various social groups that the social order is threatened, the strong against the weak. It is by wars of organized nations that modern man, armed with cold calculation and the best in weapons, marches toward the brink of ruin.

By conflict also man has been stimulated to make creative advance through the centuries with ebb and flow of fortune and settled gain. It is needless to say that all religions have been concerned with this central fact about human nature, have discerned in it that issue above all which, in all languages, calls for salvation. Man is in conflict with nature, with other men, and with himself. It is the core of his living, engaging continuously the dynamics of his being. Its dimensions are never quite the same at all times. They vary in intensity with change in inward balance and harmony with outer demands. But there is seldom absent somewhere in the background the urge of nature which Ibsen put into the mouth of the Old Man when he said to Peer Gynt, "Among men, the rule is man be thyself. Among the trolls, the rule is troll to thyself *be enough*." [4] This is not so much antithesis as the question, How much and of what kind must man be to be true to himself? Other creatures have lived the answer without ability to ask the question. To themselves, in their time, they sought to be enough and came to their end pushing their cause to its limit. Is there other course for man than to do likewise? So far as his relations with nature are concerned, the answer would be to settle the conflict by complete subjugation, by the elimination of everything that threatens him, and by conserving everything that may serve his purposes.

What the conflict with others of his kind means can be understood best by accepting nature's wisdom in giving the key position in all species to the individual and, therefore, by looking at man in the terms of his peculiar attainment as a self. We have seen how this unity of the human organism arose only after roof-brain and mind paved the way. We noted further that in its development, the self is a product of a culture whose major feature is a society of selves acting upon physical environment for common purposes and interacting with one another in intensifying and deepening the inner life. In other words, being a self is to have

---

[4] Ibsen, Henrik, *Peer Gynt*. Translation by William Charles Archer. Act II, Sc. VI, p. 71. New York: Charles Scribner's Sons, 1916. ("Troll" is an inhuman Scandinavian mythical figure.)

a mind that has internalized a culture, and to be self-conscious is to have the added property of symbolic interaction internally with what one has incorporated from others. The two inward components of the self are thus an "I" interacting with a "me," the former representing unique reactions to the external world of people and things and the latter the composite of those things in the character of their internalization.

To illustrate, all too simply, when a boy at college has spent his allowance before the next installment is due and must write home for more funds, he knows what the attitude of his parents is likely to be, and *formulates* his explanation and his need accordingly. His parents are constituents of his "me." He, in the situation of his need and the reason for exhausted funds, is his "I," but it is apparent that the two components are inseparable. For all practical purposes, the pronoun "I" covers the case. What we are saying is that it is in the nature of being a self to have a capacity for internal communication by virtue of an internalization of the roles of the people in our lives.[5] The boy could substitute the president of the college, his professors, and his friends, for his parents. He could do more than that. He could extend abstractly the internal activity by symbolization to encompass the most complicated problems of importance to him in terms of a "generalized other"

[5] A good discussion of this from a psychiatric point of view is given by L. E. Hinsie in *The Person in the Body* (W. W. Norton & Company, Inc., 1945), Chapter 4. In *The People in Your Life,* edited by Margaret M. Hughes (Alfred A. Knopf, Inc., 1952), a similar treatment of the subject appears in Chapter 3.

which might be a group of scientists or economists or historians or all humanity. These would appear representatively, and his thinking would take place in the presence of an internalized audience whose judgments he would recall or anticipate and to whom he could thinkingly give his answers. On this basis, one can imaginatively construct social contexts in terms of which he can make his claims. It is in activity of this kind that man exhibits his greatest gift, and by this criterion that we judge him to be a self with capacity for personhood.

In this account of the self, the place of the body must not be forgotten. It may be argued that the self is not identical with the body, but no one would contend that it is independent of the body. Certainly in the formation of the self, the body occupies a primary place, for it is the intimate physical environment which mediates the outer environment. This mediation is important, for the sensitivity of the body to the world of objects and other selves goes far in determining the constitution of the self. The self, like the mind, is not an organ, but it is in relation to the body as a whole in the sense in which the mind is in relation to the brain. From a genetic standpoint, it would seem that the self is built up through the experience of the mind-body organism as a social instrument. The behavior of children discloses the process. A small boy says to his playmate, "I can jump farther than you can," or "I can throw a stone farther than you can." Then he jumps and throws the stone. The playmate also jumps and throws. Here are two selves in the making, and two bodies are engaged in the

process. If the second boy's performance is better in these
acts than that of the first, there are important results for
him and for the other boy. *Success* and *failure* emerge out
of this situation, and they are associated with the effectiveness and lack of effectiveness of bodily acts. The first boy
may try again and continue practice until he brings his
body up to the challenge of his own claim, or he may give
up, or try something else more promising for putting himself in more favorable relationship with his playmate and
in his own eyes. This situation as simple and commonplace
as it may seem is a fair illustration of what, with increasing
complication, goes on in the development of the self.

A very important item in this sort of situation is the emotional accompaniment of the activity, the pleasure in success, the pain in failure. Both are objectively explicit before
the eyes of the two children in the illustration. Both measure the distance of the jump and the throw. If the winning
boy gleefully says, "See, I beat you!" the effect on the losing
boy is increased; for, in addition to his own observation of
his failure, he now has a judgment upon his act. His status
as a self is qualified by the showing of his bodily performance. In the measure of the physical failure socially judged,
his feeling about himself, his self-respect, the quality of his
self-awareness is affected. The self is constituted from activities of this sort, extending throughout the whole range of
human interest; and the body, in some degree of awareness,
is always in the situation.

If a child has persistent difficulty in socializing his body,
in integrating his experience of it with his developing self,

he may acquire feelings of shame about it. Such feelings are likely to be stronger if they flow from the behavior of parents whose handling of toilet training has been inept and whose judgments on the child's physical development have been harsh. In the resourceful child, a failure will present the challenge to improve, to rise above his record by a fighting reaction. As intimated, he may meet a particular failure on its own terms and conquer it. If this cannot be done, or better alternative presents itself, he will develop compensations through attainment in other skills. Among the latter, none is more readily at hand than accomplishment in the use of words. The self may lose in physical encounter and win honor in argument. If physical failure is marked by harsh, emotional judgments from others who are especially important to the child, or if actual physical defect puts a burden upon him, his awareness of his body may amount to a kind of rejection of it, a persistent anxiety and a resulting degree of compensation that creates, so to speak, a "bulge" on the self, an overcompensation. This makes for safety, may be socially useful, but may also present hazard to the self in later life.

In this connection one thinks, for example, of the young man who, as a child, was the only boy between two girls in the family situation. He enjoyed association with his father, but was limited in this contact because the father's occupation required his absence from home a great deal. The lad had the usual interest of the American boy in baseball, but no one to play with. Occasions when his father was at home were marked by games of pitch and toss between the two.

On one such occasion, the father threw the ball with all the strength of his right arm. The lad tried to catch it, but the force and sting of it was too much for him. When he dropped it, the father admonished, "You've got to do better than that or you will never grow up and be a man." This judgment upon the lad's failure, supported by other experiences in the family, led to a continuing anxiety which drove him to exaggerated absorption in athletics that disturbed his behavior as an adult. He felt an irrepressible urge to get on some kind of athletic team in order to demonstrate to himself that he was a man. He would choose the kind of game in which he was most proficient in order to reduce the possibility of failure. Nevertheless, no kind of game was failure-proof and, when his team lost, he would go into a tailspin of anxiety. This would be his inner state even though to an observer he was physically every inch a man even to the last whisker. The body is inescapably a part of the self, not only as its site in the natural and social order, but, more important, it provides components of experience that must be harmoniously integrated in the self.

All this is to say that culture claims the individual at the moment of birth. The work of socialization begins when the infant becomes a part of the human group and other people act upon him to shape his development. The first disciplines imposed upon him are directed toward the establishment of habits of body control. By the third year, he is expected to have these habits well ingrained. From that time forward, he becomes susceptible to an increasingly refined and balanced sort of social response. The limits are set only by his capacity for progressive adaptation; in short, his ability to learn. He must acquire manners which are first associated with the bodily function of eating. He must acquire ease in using the instruments of the table, and is made aware of acceptable and unacceptable ways of taking his food. Eventually this process becomes elaborated in the adult pattern until behavior in this area is set or stabilized. Manners soon move into other areas governing relations with persons young and old in all sorts of situations. Respect for others means restraint upon oneself; consideration for others means a further adjustment of the self to other selves in bodies, their needs and rights, and so on to the end of the adult chapter.

Growth and mastery of social relations, vastly enhanced by language, develops in the child eventually a character consisting of habits, attitudes, and ideas by which he knows himself. He learns from situations in which he finds himself inadequate and responds to the need to improve. Normally in time, having been exposed to the demands of a variety of situations in which the reactions of others are reflected back to him, and experiencing the support of identifications with those to whom he inwardly relates himself, he develops confidence and feels a sense of freedom or readiness to meet future situations. This confidence and freedom dynamically structured are among the marks of a competent human being, and both arrive by the disciplines of progressive socialization in a culture that is at once prod and guide. Thus the body is not an end in itself, but an instrument for participation in social activities. One measure of the maturity of the self is the degree in which one is free from deliberate preoccupation with the body. This freedom is possible because responses to the needs of the body are organized in habit and, therefore, require a minimum of voluntary thought-out attention, leaving the main energies of the mind and self to be invested in social concerns of the *person*. Even in eating, good table talk diverts attention from the fact that one is feeding himself. In organic illness, the body presents a problem, and the self has the body, for the time being at least, "on its hands" without recourse except to wait for recovery.

3. *Deeper Levels of the Internal Life*

The commonsense account which we have been following can be expressed in other ways. Sigmund Freud is a name to conjure with in modern attempts to understand human nature. He was a physician who, at the beginning of his career, approached the problem of man committed to an effort to explain all phenomena of mind in terms of strict biology. Out of his experience in treating mental disease, he developed a system of concepts and techniques which have come to be known as psychoanalysis.

The motive that led Freud to pursue his investigation was the observation that impairment in the use of a physical organ by a patient can occur apart from any diagnostic evidence of physiological deterioration in the organ itself. His studies led to the discovery that the cause of the illness lay outside of the body in a life situation of the patient which induced a strong emotional conflict that sought out-let in the pathological symptom. The patient was unaware of any such connection. He complained only of the symp-tom. To explain the event, Freud posited the existence of forces operating in the patient outside his field of aware-ness or consciousness. He called this the unconscious. In time he elaborated other concepts to round out a system within whose framework the diagnosis of mental aberration could be understood and treated. Proceeding from the two major divisions of mind into conscious and unconscious, he added the co-conscious and pre-conscious to express inter-mediate states. He distinguished also between the ego and the id, the one representing the consciously accepted or-ganized self in direct contact with reality, the other repre-senting mainly the level of instinctual impulse and prim-itive reactions to early experience. The latter, being unacceptable to the ego, are repressed or forced out of the field of awareness.

Freud also introduced the idea of the superego to desig-nate the action of conscience and ideals having their source in society in reinforcing the ego's activity in repression.[6] All these names and functions ultimately did duty for the libido or the energy factor in personality. He conceived this to be primarily sexual, but his orientation was broader than the physical demands of sex in the make-up of the in-

---

[6] Freud's idea of conscience is not the same as that which we de-veloped in connection with our discussion of Moses in Chapter 1. There conscience is the internal reaction to justice in social relations. The two concepts must not be confused.

dividual. The sexual included social experiences with the sexes, especially the early relations of children to their parents giving rise to oedipus situations involving attachment of the boy, in the unconscious, to the mother with rivalry feelings toward the father and, similarly, attachment of the girl to her father with rivalry feelings toward the mother. These are hurdles which have to be made in the psychosexual development of the individual. Failure to make them tends to issue in emotional problems that may become causes of restriction or illness. This brief statement by no means exhausts the elaborate system which Freud and his followers built to guide the practice of psychoanalysis.[7] There have been protests from responsible critics outside the school and strong, dissenting voices within it, resulting in modifications of original presuppositions and greater emphasis upon cultural factors. Though the terms used have their main meaning in the system and have the same status in explaining mental life as protons, electrons, and neutrons have in understanding physical phenomena, they have contributed much to our knowledge of human dynamics, more perhaps in the sense of the value of the empirical data accumulated from the practice of the system than from the merits of the system itself. The basic concepts, however, are firmly established.

A fairly clear conception of the working of the unconscious in relation to everyday life may be gained from a

---

[7] A good interpretation of Freud's views has recently appeared in a book by Calvin S. Hall entitled *A Primer of Freudian Psychology,* published by the World Publishing Company of Cleveland, Ohio.

hypothetical illustration. Imagine three men entering a florist shop. All are attracted by some roses on display. The first man looks at them very carefully. Soon we notice a light in his eye and an intense expression on his face. He lifts out one rose from the vase. He is inwardly excited, inquires from the clerk where it came from and seeks such other information as he can get, and then rushes off. He is an expert on roses. He knows he has found a mutation, something new under the sun in roses. He takes it eagerly to his laboratory for examination. Observing this man's action and knowing what it is all about, we would say that his behavior is perfectly normal. We expect a botanist to be interested in flowers and to cherish new types which appear.

The errand of the second man is different. His wedding anniversary is at hand, and he has come to buy a dozen roses to be sent to his wife. This action, we would say, is also normal, at least for husbands who have a memory for anniversaries. Our culture says that when we have something nice to say, to say it with flowers, so this man's action does not detain us.

The third man, however, startles us by his reaction to roses. He cannot tolerate them. Their fragrance nauseates him. He avoids them as he would the plague. This strikes us as peculiar in the light of the normal expectations of customary reaction to roses. If we ask him why he does not like roses, he will not be able to tell us. Likely he will say, "I just don't like them. All my life, I have not liked them." But we know that there must be a reason for such an aversion, so we ask him to tell us something about his past life. He is talkative and mentions many things, most of which have nothing to do with roses. Then, almost incidentally, he tells us that his mother died when he was four years old. Now we feel that we are on a warm trail, and we try to help him tell us more about her death. It is difficult. He doesn't remember much, and soon wanders off on other things. But we are persistent. Quietly and as skillfully as we can, we keep taking him back toward that lost scene. We ask about the house he lived in at the time; what his father's work was; were there other children; how old they were; was he the baby, and who came to take care of him; did his father remarry, and so on.

After many attempts, and perhaps a very long process, we get the whole story from this third man. For the first time since that day long ago, he recalls the room in which his mother lay with a great blanket of roses spread over her casket. Now we know, and he knows too, why he has no tolerance for roses. His mother's death was such a great loss to him that he could not bear to remember it. He put it out of his mind. He repressed it. Life went on, but the injury was unhealed. As a grown man, symbolically and irrationally, he blamed the flowers for his buried grief and fled from them without knowing why. In a similar manner, phobias, obsessions, compulsive acts of various types appear to distort the behavior of many people. Like the man and the roses, they learn to live with these survivals of their past and are not too disabled by them, but their freedom and enjoyments are curtailed by as much as the restriction imposes.

It should not be concluded from this illustration, or from Freud's teaching, that the unconscious is involved only in the distortion of the ego's response to reality. Quite to the contrary. It is an integral part of our minds and serves us more in solving problems than in creating them. Often, in fact, after struggling consciously to find the answer to an important question we give up and go out to play a game of golf or do something else to rest our minds. After our shower at the clubhouse, or on our return from some other avocation, the answer to our question flashes into consciousness. Some of our most important discoveries in science have been made in this way, and everybody has had the experience of a sudden "inspiration" that was the solution to a puzzling problem. The answer would not come because the tension produced by working directly on the problem shut out the resources on the deeper levels of the mind. When one gives up or relaxes, "unconscious cerebration" or "the living residue of past experience" gives the appropriate response.[8]

This aspect of the mind's working is especially manifest in dreams which Freud did so much to help us understand. Another illustration will serve our purpose here. A young minister found himself developing strong feelings of hostility toward an older minister who was a "commanding figure" in the denomination to which the former belonged.

---

[8] Herrick, C. J., *The Thinking Machine*, p. 277. Chicago: University of Chicago Press, 1929.

Contact in every setting where these two men met was occasion for the younger man inwardly to feel critical and hostile. Sometimes he expressed these feelings to others. In time, however, he became concerned about them for there was no basis for them in fact. The older minister not only had never harmed the young man in any way but had frequently shown him special favor. In this lay the puzzle. The younger man determined to bring his feelings into line with reality. He tried to force himself and failed. He prayed about the matter. One day he took pen and paper and wrote down a complete list of the accomplishments of the older man, all the things he and everybody else admired in the man. This helped some but did not remove the old feelings. The internal struggle went on for some months. Then, one day, the younger man received a letter from a denominational executive asking him to serve on a committee of which the older man was the chairman. His reaction was immediate. He threw the letter on his desk with the thought that his answer was going to be "No!" He did nothing more than that at the time.

That night the young minister had a dream. In the dream he was in his own church and pulpit. A great throng of people was gathered to hear him. They were standing. The farther walls seemed to be nonexistent. The edge of the crowd disappeared into shadowy space. Everybody was smiling with uplifted faces toward the young preacher. He described the scene by saying, "It was like a sea of smiles." Soon there was a disturbance on the dim periphery of the "congregation." The older minister appeared from nowhere and made his way forward through the crowd toward the altar. There was no aisle in the church of the dream. The older man was also smiling in his usual warm, friendly manner. Arrived at the front he put out his hand to take the hand of the man in the pulpit. The dream ended there. All of it, of course, was a momentary flash, much briefer than the space it takes to report it in words.

This dream presented to the young minister what was hidden from his conscious "eye." The imagery in it shows that it is closer to the reality situation than many dreams which employ a "forgotten language," to use Erich Fromm's suggestive phrase. The effort of the young man to solve his problem needed only to be supplemented by the added information that came to him while he slept. As he studied it and discussed it, he saw the humor which pervaded it. He was the "big man" in the pulpit. He was receiving the adulation of a larger congregation than he had ever addressed in his waking experience. In fact, it seemed that the "whole world was there." There was standing room only! The "commanding figure" was pushing everybody aside to reach the altar and shake hands after the manner of a sinner accepting salvation. The friendliness of everybody toward him was really the way the young minister consciously wanted to feel himself, but he experienced the opposite instead, unless he was in the position of dominance. As he worked through the material with other amplifications, he saw also in the older man an authority figure disclosing some of his boyhood feelings toward his father.

With such clarifications as these, the young man attained insight with excellent result. He accepted appointment on the committee, and his feelings toward the older man became positive and sincerely appreciative. It would be wrong to conclude from this example that dreams tell the whole truth about a person. They do tell much and go far. Probably the main fact is that the unconscious mind speaks in the dream to the conscious saying something like this, "There is more in this business than you think. This is the way the picture looks down here. Better consider it." Joseph's dreams revealed to his brothers what manner of man he was and they did not like it. When disguises are removed, dreams tend to be brutally frank, but they are for our salvation.

These illustrations utilize the conception of the unconscious which Freud developed, but that does not mean that it is dependent entirely upon the Freudian system. The concept of the unconscious is of general application, and may be used in any relevant setting of observation and interpretation. What we really did in the illustrations was to indicate that present behavior is always in continuity with the person's past which includes all the adaptations he has made to the demands of life. These survive to affect his adjustment positively or negatively in his current situation.

4. *Prospect Beyond Science for Self and Person*

From a commonsense point of view, enlightened by insights from the sciences, our conception of the self as "I" joined

with "me" provides a pattern of understanding comparable to that of any other system.[9] The "me" includes the
body in all its divisions of labor and physiological functioning, perceived as a whole by the mind collaborating with
the brain. It includes all past events in which the individual has been involved from the time of conception to
adulthood. The "me" is the repository of external events
internalized, first by the conditioned reflex of the neuromuscular organism, then, after the acquisition of speech,
by a process of symbolization vastly extending its range.
The "I" emerges with awareness of the body differentiated
from other bodies; then, as we said, with developing perception of other selves having minds revealed through symbols. The "me" is object. The "I" is subject. The two components of the soul interact, the "I" communicating with
the "me" which, in its total character, stands for society.

Through the "me," the "I" can recall its past by reliving
symbolically situations, events it has experienced from early
childhood when it began to know itself and the world until
the most recent yesterday. What is new in the "I" today
becomes a part of the "me" tomorrow. The "I," from the
time of its emergence, reshapes the "me," molds the external event, adapts it to ends and purposes that serve further
experience. The "I" is the spearhead of the conscious self
using as support the deposits of the past in the "me." The

---

[9] In the account which we are giving at this point, we are following
in part the work of George H. Mead in his *Mind, Self and Society*.
Copyright 1934 by The University of Chicago. Used by permission.

"I" knows the "me" as "mine," the body and the world adapted for the adventure of personal living.

So the boy in our previous illustration, by co-ordination of mind and hand in selecting the stone and the use of muscular energy in throwing it, is more than the sum of all these elements. He is a self, affected reflexively by the motor act, a self succeeding or failing in the presence of other selves with accompanying feelings about the act that is *his*. Likewise our man at the lathe, with narrowed attention to a single complicated operation, is more than a worker named by his motor acts. He, too, is a self knowing his being as person through communication with other persons— wife and children, friends and fellow workers, and the wide world as far as he can see, think, and feel.

Looking back upon our total past with such imagination as we can bring to fact, we see that primordial "day" when life emerged, mayhap some protein molecule and enzyme; the cell using these, association of cells into colonies, elaboration of life in systems surging on their way on a thousand fronts, some coming to their end, others going on until man, on one branch of the life tree, came with foot shaped to stand erect, roof-brain, free hand, then mind, then self; each, in turn, drawing upon processes tried and tested, surrendering what was no longer needed, and then transcending all that had gone before. If there is a law in all this, if there is a basic uniformity that generalizes the whole operation, it is the law of recapitulation and transcendence, and man is in its grip. He may work with it or he may work against it. In so far as he has reshaped nature, his success is the result of working with it. Now he must transcend himself. The life he bears and knows must go on to something higher, fuller, better. This is the problem of man as it has been, is now, and will continue to be. This is religion, for religion in any language that articulates the main issue is self-transcendence. The statement requires no proof. It is self-evident to all who are capable of perceiving even the most elementary meanings of human existence in the context of events which have taken place on this planet and are now in course.

For the most part, in our thinking thus far, we have been "reading out" of the record as we saw it, not without bias and limitation of current purpose but we believe with real sense. Now the time has come to "read into" the record, then "out" again. This is the procedure of most attempts to grasp meanings from the past, to see them in the character of the original event, to discern the degree of their relevance to our interests in a different setting, then to use the resulting insight for further purpose. Else what is the use of pursuing knowledge in any form? It must be admitted that man is an incurable anthropizer if one may employ a word without standing in common speech. What it means goes without saying. Anyone can examine the evidence for the human tendency to make the world over in forms that stamp the human character upon it. The neolithic implement and the jet rocket shooting through the air at the speed of sound are anthropist to the final touch of finger and tool. Man spreads himself over the face of nature to shape her to his purposes in order that he may be more himself as man.

A young biochemist in his laboratory, asked what light he could throw on how the nonliving became the living, replied, "We speak only of what our tools and methods can accomplish and of that not yet. One guess is that as the primeval vapors settled into slowly cooling, earth-girdling seas, sheets of recurrent lightning impregnated microscopic particles in the heavy air with electricity. These settled into the warm water as latent life." He smiled at the thought. He was working at the time with proteins. Asked what he could tell about the remarkable properties of the protein molecule, he said, "Ah, that's what puzzles us. We're still working on it." Scientist to the nth degree, believing no "guesses" until fact sustained them, checking with instruments of precision to make sure that no bias, wish, or fancy corrupted his results, with reverence for things as they are, this young man was anthropist to his fingertips. His laboratory, work of many minds, hands, and machines, arranged according to the disciplines of his craft, was the place of his rendezvous with a slice of nature eager to deliver its secrets when he is man enough to receive them. He will first read out of nature what he finds there, then into her his symbols and formulae; then, by his or other hands, he will change nature, adapt her ways a little more to heart's desire with the imprint of his image upon them. It is inevitable that man should anthropize everything he sees and touches, sometimes crudely and clumsily, at other times with subtlety and refinement, and every such attainment reacts upon him to make him something other than he was. The "I" supported by all the "mes" it has incorporated stands frontiersman on the border of the ordered wilderness that is unfathomed nature with zest to push the conquest to the ultimate of possibilities which stand now only at fair beginning.

He would be shocked to hear it, but the young scientist's guess about the origin of life sounds strangely like a word at the beginning of an ancient book:

> The earth was without form and void, and darkness was upon the face of the deep; and the Spirit of God was moving over the face of the waters. And God said, "Let there be light"; and there was light.[10]

The context of the two sayings are wide apart and their meanings are not interchangeable, but the two speakers are one in one respect. Both are selves bending nature to the order of personhood on the latest frontier of earth. Each is agent of advance not possible before, and when that advance, by the travail of time and circumstance arrives as a fulfillment, the entire past appears in new light as though by revelation. It is thus that man in the dimension of mind discovers purpose where purpose could not be read before and, in the dimension of self, discovers God as supreme Spirit inviting him to seek fulfillment by self-transcendence in final personhood. By faith, man, as scientist, pushes back the frontiers of nature for fuller appropriation of her powers for his purposes. By faith, man, as person, yields

---

10 Genesis 1:2,3. (RSV)

himself to ever hopeful progression under the advancing disciplines of the God who made him a little higher than the apes and a little lower than the angels.

A distinguished biologist has well stated the outlook of the scientist in evaluating the contribution of ideals and values to the future of the race. We quote what he says:

> Aspirations do influence the course of events. Thoughts, ideals, purposes are among the determining factors for happenings in nature. It is not strictly true that "popular approval or disapproval will not alter the course of nature" if man is a part of nature. The desires and aspirations of humanity are determiners in the operation of the universe on the same footing with physical determiners. What is to come in the future is not predictable from what has occurred in the past. The laws of nature are not immutable in the sense that new laws shall not be exemplified as new conditions arise. Because things have occurred in a certain way in the past, it does not follow that they must occur in the future. . . . There is nothing in legitimate science or scientific method that makes it unreasonable to hope for the appearance in the future of what has not been seen in the past. Nothing in science is incompatible with striving to realize ideals that have never yet been realized.[11]

What, however, is the discipline which man may deliberately adopt in seeking solution to the problem posed by his nature? How may he take charge of himself and work out his destiny, in so far as that depends on his choice of

---

[11] Jennings, H. S., *The Biological Basis of Human Nature*, p. 376. New York: W. W. Norton and Company, Inc., 1930. Used by permission.

means? We shall look for the answer to these questions by returning to the individual human being who, as product of biology and culture, is the source of all new beginnings in history. What we saw concretely in the experiences of biblical man we may now set in the perspective of that consummation of inner event which offers promise of a more reasoned future for mankind.

8. RELIGION AND PSYCHOTHERAPY

1. *Man's Destiny as Person*

> *Religion is the art and the theory of the internal life of man so far as that de-pends on the man himself and on what is permanent in the nature of things.*
> —ALFRED NORTH WHITEHEAD

THE CHARACTER OF RELIGIOUS ACTIVITY could not be stated more accurately or more in accord with history. Religion is the supreme and autonomous interest of man in his quest to attain the utmost possibility of himself as person through reliance upon God. All other interests of his highly diversified life come together in the final questions pertaining to what kind of character and conduct expresses his full dignity and what destiny is appropriate to his powers.

The core of religion pertains to values and beliefs of a peculiar character, well illustrated by the Sermon on the Mount, grounded in a world view that supports man's pursuit of them with his highest intelligence and devotion.

They are integral with man himself as his destiny is read in the light of his place in nature and his potentiality for further development. All other values resulting from partial pursuits of vocation and avocation are subordinate and tributary to the central issue of man's relation to God and the outcomes of his achievement under God. The special importance of Jesus lies in the culmination in him of man's search for that in his life which is permanent or eternal, that objective of living which, when grasped and given control in human conduct, directs his effort toward the best that ever can be. For those of Christian persuasion, Jesus expresses for all time that detachment from limited and secondary values which enables men clearly to see where the main course of their adventure lies. They know that they cannot take the road back, though the burdens which they bear often tempt them to make such retreat. They know that there is no standing still. The energy of life itself cries for expenditure. An insatiable curiosity to understand and exploit nature, with the new incentive for exploration that comes with every discovery, makes it impossible for man to hold to his tracks. Forward is the road sign that catches attention and elicits intelligent response. Nevertheless, the way ahead is always fraught with blockages, false trails, wrong decisions, and costly failures. History is replete with evidence that man is not the rational creature he is wont to be or that, in his better moods, he knows himself to be. He learns slowly, is apt in repeating his errors, funds little of his hard-earned gains in any age for future generations. His deposits of yesterday's knowledge are empty until experience of today refills them. Few human problems are permanently solved and such as appear to be at one time issue new challenge as settings change. New occasions call for decisions set in their own terms while increasing complexities alter the dimensions of action.

Living and having his being in association with his kind, inevitably subject to dynamics that are the substance and order of his nature, man's greatest need is served by objectives beyond himself providing perspective on any given situation with values that control and guide. This is the function of religion offering in each situation principles for the integration of diverse claims, discriminating among the worthy and less worthy, the better and the worse, and presenting goals that at once liberate from division and decay and mobilize resources for disciplined advance. These principles and values with their meanings are the furnishings of the "internal life." These, as we saw them in the Bible, may now be related to psychology for the further clarification of our conception of man as person and its consequent implications for the practice of religion.

In the last days of the old commonwealth of Israel, as hope faded under internal division and external attack, there emerged a few great individuals—men with broken hearts to match the fragments of social decay around them. They had a faith that penetrated the far horizons of future possibility. They refused to admit that the end had come. The ruins around them were envisioned as foundations for a new superstructure which a surviving remnant consecrated under God would build. But such reconstruction in their view was not to have existence as wood and stone. Their similes, metaphors, oracles, and parables, using physical objects and concrete situations, spoke of the spirit and of life. The bones left from yesterday's anguish would be reclothed with new flesh and ensouled for further march up the centuries. The older law, not outmoded, but shifted into the background because the social order it sustained no longer existed, would be superseded by a law written upon the heart. The voice that would give encouragement and direction would not come from the thunders of Sinai, the earthquake, wind, or fire, but in the strength of man's inward resolution would open a door of hope in the valley of Achor.[1] It was in the capacity of these individuals to transcend self, to strike hands over chaos with the God of history, that again saw end become beginning. The light shone in the darkness, and a man became the shadow of a great rock in a weary land. Multitudes whose minds were clouded by disaster, whose hearts melted and whose spirits drooped to the lowland and the depths of the valley, drifted into oblivion while the prophet spoke from the mountain of vision of the day of the Lord. It has always been so, and it remains the key to our times. The individual is the unit of the world from the lowest of the orders to the highest. It is in him that adventure is reborn, sustained, and communicated to others for turning their flagging steps into courageous march.

So it was in the days when Jesus came. Again it was the

---

[1] Hosea 2:15. "And there will I give her her vineyards and make the Valley of Achor a door of hope." (RSV) Cf. Joshua 7:24-26.

Great Individual, this time the supreme Person, announcing a beginning when all around him were signs of the end; when leaders were idealizing a dead past, straining out the gnat and swallowing the camel, compromising with the worst to make life tolerable for themselves, and the common people languished in poverty and oppression, sheep without a shepherd. From Galilee of the Gentiles, suspect as source of any good thing, he strode up and down the little land of his fathers, enclave between desert and sea, battleground of the nations with eroded hills that rose from the valley of death to greet their primeval origin in the stars beyond the Milky Way. The carpenter's tools were laid aside for the building of rooms of the spirit in the Father's house.

"Follow me," Jesus said, and the day of new march began. With "immeasurable innocence," which the worldly-wise could not understand and even his disciples at their best could only distort, he spoke. In him, a dead world came alive as he drew pictures to quicken imagination, to reveal the hidden glory of life and open the graves of buried hopes. The multitudes gathered around him, but it was always to the individual that he spoke. The blessed are the poor in spirit, the mourning, the merciful, those who hunger and thirst after righteousness, the pure in heart. Among these each man found himself. The sinner to him was always an individual with responsibility and power for initiative no matter what his condition might be. There was no nurturing of dependency in Jesus' teaching, no lifting of the load every man must carry. In childlike simplicity

he spoke to maturity. He opened the storehouse of suffi-
ciency that every man might stand upon his own feet, walk
and not faint, for it is in the seeking and decision of the
individual for the better that is presently before him that
the kingdom comes.

Jesus knows no such fiction as the "mass mind" as indeed
there is none, any more than there is a mass brain. He perceives and accepts people as they are. It is in his touch with
children, the "little ones" without claim of status, the sick,
the sinning publican and the betrayed woman, those in
whom personhood is on the make but threatened, that he
appears in the full stature of love. Only unbelief, the hardened heart of finished creed and the dullness of sated selfish-
ness, could close the gate opening full upon the disciplined
but ample way leading to increasing liberation from the
older forms of a low sheltered past into another day of adventure.

Faith, in Jesus' view, is not credulity nor wanton ram-
bling of vagrant thought. It is not pursuing the will-o'-the-
wisp of some Utopian dream, or trusting in the magic of
autosuggestion. It is opening the mind to possibility, cal-
culating the risks and taking them like the general who
before battle took account of whether he could with ten
thousand meet the enemy coming with twenty thousand.
Faith, for Jesus, is always the first step in action; but the
rub comes in the blindness of preoccupation that shuts out
or limits the perception of possibility. There men stumble
more than at any other point. The old trails are known,
traveled and retraveled. They are grooved in the brain, set-

tled in the formulae. *Ne plus ultra,* they say. So life grows
stale, and creeping death takes its toll of the human spirit.
But if one has as much faith as a grain of mustard seed,
the smallest measure of possibility, how great may be the
results! A little crack in the old shell can be the end of one
world and the beginning of another. And when we see these
attitudes in Jesus in the perspective of the knowledge of our
day, a million years leap to confirm him. Faith, "calculat-
ing" possibility and pressing it to the limit with courage to
fail and ingenuity to try again, marks the trail from star-
dust to man. For Jesus, however, it was enough to say,
"With God, all things are possible." And he said that thinking about a young man who, admitting his lack, halted at
the doorway through which he might have passed beyond
self into the fuller stature of personhood.

2. *Christian Psychotherapy and the Nurture of Personhood*

Religion integral with life at its best involves change in
orientation and direction of inward purpose issuing in
decision which moves ever nearer to personal wholeness in
God. It is more than integration of personality in the psychological sense, though that is an indispensable part of the
process. It is integration with the addition of integrity or
the rightness of a relationship with God sealed by trust. In
this context our conception of psychotherapy emerges. The
word stresses a kind of action or influence that is exerted
to meet the need of the "soul" or the functioning of a man

as a person. It is a kind of activity directed toward the elimination of a deficiency and the corrective rebuilding of inner attitudes that have gone astray or have set limits to the full functioning of the individual. The term is capable of the narrowed meaning associated with the use of technically refined psychological methods that lie outside the formal operations of religion.[2] All that is excluded from our present concern. We are thinking of psychotherapy in its most native and historic association with religion as the name for the process by which a self becomes a person and grows into maturity through remedial change or redemption. It involves understandings of personality derived from our most secure knowledge of man, but all such knowledge is a tool to advance the purpose of personal wholeness in the values which justify and direct human action. Christian psychotherapy, in the very naming of it, involves that frame of reference supplied by the meanings of biblical faith in the presence of which personhood comes to issue, its deficiency or bondage to self is disclosed, and redemptive healing is indicated.

With this orientation we may now bring to final focus the distinction which we have been making between self and person, selfhood and personhood. Earlier we described the human individual as a biosocial organism, as a "me" joined with an "I," composed of body, internalized social

---

[2] In Chapter I of their book, *The Process of Psychotherapy*, H. V. Ingham and L. R. Love refer to psychotherapy in the broad terms of a "cultural institution" which has emerged in response to anxiety-producing social changes of our time. New York: McGraw-Hill Book Company, Inc., 1954.

experience, and *reaction to that experience*. Selfhood, then, would be the quality of the total response of the "I" in social situations where the terms are set by other selves and the action expected is agreement or conformity. But the "I" has another orientation related to further development and fulfillment through elaboration and transcendence of strict social command. It seeks to accomplish this by an internal dialogue which symbolically projects alternatives of meaning and action. As a result, it may choose to conform or to create a different response by bringing together elements of the self in a form not previously expressed. This capacity for divergent behavior, in the achievement of personhood, has both positive and negative aspects. Maladaptation in the structure of the self may give rise to antisocial conduct on the part of the person or cause him to retreat into illness. On the other hand, when the variation is grounded in an integrated self, a new pattern of reaction may contribute to constructive social change. Our sequence in the scheme of life then becomes cell, body, brain, mind, self, person. Mead's "generalized other," as internal surrogate for society, and Freud's concept of the superego are drawn to the terms of the social origin and function of the self. They fail to give full account of the universe of possibility outside and beyond the options of any achieved social order. In other words, when a man's thought and action are reoriented by the extension of concern to actualize what is not contained in the inheritance of the self, yet is relevant to current condition and future possibility, we judge him to be acting as a person.

This is the fact which brings the meaning of religion into full perspective. It is the same meaning which we saw in our study of the soul of Israel, particularly in the work of the prophets, Jesus, and Paul. There the central issue was *belief* in the action of God in shaping events, His concern that man should survive misfortune and decay, and continuously renew his adventure by rediscovering himself in every crisis that emerged. This was the "word of the Lord" uttered by the prophets and reaffirmed by Jesus on the mount of temptation. "Man shall not live by bread alone but by every word which proceeds out of the mouth of God."

Thus the contrast is drawn between men conversing with one another as persons on the level of mutual *self*-interest and men communicating with God in search of ultimate fulfillment and their consequent resolution to serve that end in their current tasks. This concern is expressed by beliefs which relate the local and the temporal to the universal and the timeless and which invest human action with a dimension that transcends particular occasions. At their minimum, the characteristic marks of a religious man are his perception of his involvement in everything human, his formulation of the meaning of this involvement, and his commitment, in joint effort with others, to a course of responsible action judged to be in accord with his most intelligent understanding of the purpose of God. It is by beliefs so derived and shared that man inwardly sustains himself as autonomous person under God, in disengagement from obsessive preoccupation with immediate demands, and stretches creative imagination to encompass the vision of eternal truth and righteousness.

It was this sense of vocation which pervaded the history of Israel from Abraham to Paul and reached culmination in the concept of the Servant in the Old Testament and the concept of the Saviour in the New. This was also that self-denial which Jesus defined as the condition of discipleship and added to it the promise of the higher freedom which comes from losing one's life and finding it again in devotion to an all-absorbing cause. This, too, was a part of the scene on Golgotha where the meaning of self-renunciation was set forth in unforgettable terms and followed by the resurrection faith declaring the triumph of God's act for all men in the *person* of Jesus Christ. It was in the majesty of cosmic loneliness, when all earthly supports were withdrawn, that the Man of Galilee achieved the autonomy of Divine Man. To live with this orientation, uniting in balance the trinity of *me-I-Thou,* is to find release from the restricting anxieties of self-concern and of that egocentricity which so often lies at the source of mental illness.[3] This, indeed, is the straight and narrow way and few there are who attain unto the discipline of it. The fact remains, however, that it is in relation to God that man comes to full awareness of himself as person and is able to respond to the

[3] That religious beliefs which in their better form sustain man in his dignity as person may, by virtue of defects in the constitution of the self, become delusions and hallucinations is well documented by Anton T. Boisen's *Exploration of the Inner World* (New York: Harper & Brothers, 1936), and more recently by Wayne Oates' *Religious Factors in Mental Illness* (New York: Association Press, 1954).

activity of God in the redemption of self and society. Personhood, in the religious sense, refers, therefore, to that quality of the soul which is peculiarly the work of God in completing His creation in man.

In the light of this reasoning, it is worthy of note that theologians, in their thought about God, have almost uniformly used the concept of person. Rarely have they spoken of Him as a self. Even so, they have encountered difficulty in describing the nature of Divine Being because the limited and concrete character of the human person makes it appear that God bears the image of man when precisely the opposite is meant. That difficulty is surmounted, in part at least, by thinking of the personhood of God, for then we stress only what we are capable of identifying in Him as sovereign creator of persons through His use of the emergent "I," the spearhead of self-consciousness manifest in formulated faith or belief.

This outlook has important bearing on the meaning of love. In the two great commandments, the emphasis is placed on loving God with all one's mind, heart, soul, and strength, and one's neighbor as oneself. In this we may recognize two kinds of love, or love expressed at two different levels. There is the love which takes the form of reciprocal act between selves. It involves an exchange of benefits or mutual support in a particular and limited social relationship. Sometimes this is colloquially called "trader love" which says, in effect, "You give it to me and I will return it to you." This kind of love is very useful in human relations. It has its origin in the exchange of affection between parent and child and is indispensable in the early integration of the self. Much of the social business of adult life is also stabilized by this kind of love. Neighborly attitudes and acts contribute to security and strengthen relationships for common undertakings.

When, however, Jesus unites the two commandments, he adds another dimension to love. It is clear that the love of God is not the love of a self and that human love toward God is made possible by our own personhood. The emphasis upon the necessity for wholeheartedness in this love accentuates the limitation which arises from the content and finitude of the self, on the one hand, and its need to be transformed, on the other. Personal self-love then becomes the condition for entering into mutuality with others at the level of God's interest in man. Thus, by loving ourselves as persons in the making under God, we may love others in the same manner and for the same reason. But this love is active at any time and in any social relationship only in the degree in which we have attained personhood. Those who may be more mature in this love than others must give their strength to the less mature as parent to child. It is in this context that Christian psychotherapy attains relevance, for it expresses the need for continuous inward healing or reconstruction of attitudes and involves more than episodic treatment required by some acute situation of conflict or illness. Christian psychotherapy is needed in every situation where there is crisis for personhood, and that means in every important decision. Hence the need for the ministry and the church in continuous functional relationship with developing persons.

The word "person," very aptly chosen to designate a human being, has a twofold connotation. It is derived from the Latin *persona* and refers to the "mask" worn by actors on the stage where they appear in character other than their own. The second and more basic meaning is "to sound through" or a "sound coming through." Under the first conception, we may place all that goes by the name of psychological defenses, those barriers erected by inhibition and repression against primitive impulses. The child, in his adaptation to his life situation, discovers that certain types of behavior are disapproved. They are expressions of his natural feelings and a part of his exploration of reality. But he wants to be comfortable and happy among others, to get along with his parents, teachers, and friends, so he casts himself in their role. He puts on a mask, so to speak. It is very important to understand this process.

The other meaning of the word is equally significant, for it stresses the fact that the chief attribute of a person is capacity for communication. One of the main tests of mental soundness is whether speech is intact or not. We speak of a man being coherent or incoherent or the degree in which he is either. These two facts about a person provide the principal clue to the method of psychotherapy. It involves penetrating the defenses behind which lurk attitudes and feelings that affect inward balance and outer freedom. The process of it is "talking out," or bringing the offending complex into the open, inspecting it and reassimilating it to one's pattern of living. But the religious man knows that a mask is useless. Like Hagar in the wilderness he feels under the survey of the all-seeing eye of Another. Consequently one might just as well tell God what one thinks of Him, as Job did, as to have the thoughts and not utter them. The presumption is that before God a man is what he is. The bare recognition of this does not, however, lead to the solution of a problem. It may accentuate it. For further light on the subject we turn again to the Bible.

3. *The Bible and Insight*

The main value of the Scriptures does not lie in the formal doctrines which may be derived from them with the result, sometimes, of reducing their vitality. Their abiding worth subsists in the fact that they disclose a wide range for observing the human mind in engagement with reality. Expressed in language and literary forms native to their times, they succeed without trying in presenting human nature with a realism probably unmatched in any other literature.

The modern psychoanalyst with his patient on the couch, probing the unconscious, will not find there anything essentially unlike the primitive emotions boldly acted out in the Bible. Sex is there in its shame and in its glory. Incest, harlotry, rape, prostitution as a religious rite are mingled with sexual imagery in the most elevated thoughts. The seductive Delilah delivers the giant, Samson, into the hands of his enemies. David sees Bathsheba in her bath and orders her husband killed that he may have her. The resourceful

Rebekah, the beloved Rachel, the devout Hannah nurturing her little son for the Lord, the "virgin" who is so often a figure of destiny in the visions of the prophets, and Hosea's remarkable parable of the love of God for Israel set forth in his own experience of taking a harlot for a wife and loving her—all these are mere samples of the wholesome in sex standing alongside the sordid. As for aggression, deception, intrigue, and blood revenge, one need only mention the fratricide of Cain, the brutality of Joab, the shrewdness of Jacob, and the conspiracy of Absalom. Loyalty flowers forth in the charming pastoral idyl of Ruth while love crosses the boundaries of race. Romance dances with lilting phrase in the Song of Songs. Protest against prejudice and bigotry is posted in Nineveh by Jonah while hate finds outlet in Esther, Nahum, and the imprecatory Psalms. Through all these scenes, however, there is resolute effort to inhibit the instincts, to balance good and evil, first by the law of tooth for tooth and eye for eye, then by moral judgments substituting mercy and kindness for greed, and finally by hedging in the sacred with ritual and ceremony.

In the New Testament the setting is different, but human frailty is no less conspicuous. The fickle Peter, doubting Thomas, the subversive Judas, the desperate Paul belong to the ranks of common men giving consent to the better in their nature qualified by the weaker and the worse. On the heights, one stands with Jeremiah and Second Isaiah, or braves the inner tumult of Ezekiel's groping for a word that comes to terms with an intolerable situation. In all this, one supreme fact stands out. Divinity does not flee from humanity or leave it in the dust. The God of Israel, though fenced in by his people, works at his task in the rough and tumble of the human heart. He is too holy to avoid the unholy. He will take the crude stuff of man, one step from the jungle, and make him into a person. So Jesus consorts with publicans and sinners, takes shifting sand that was a fisherman and molds it into a "rock," captures a zealot on the road to Damascus and changes the inner flame to the steady glow of a light for the Gentiles.

The Bible is a hall of mirrors in which we may see the reflection of every kind of human emotion that we know in ourselves. With Paul we see self in a glass darkened by infantile wishes and fancies and then, discovering maturity in the transcendent love of personhood in which we know ourselves as we "are known," we "put away childish things." In the Psalms particularly, collected in the latter days of Israel when the national spirit turned inward, the sweep of feeling is almost unlimited. In Psalm 137 we sit with the captives by the waters of Babylon while our captors torment us by asking for a song to entertain them and we place a curse on them, blessing anyone who will take their children and dash them against a stone. From that we rise to Psalm 139 where, in majestic scene, Omnipresent Spirit finds us where we are and we cry, "Search me, O God, and know my heart! Try me and know my thoughts!" In Psalm 23 we yield to the inward calm that comes from the Shepherd God who leads us into green pastures and beside still waters restoring the soul. On the notes of this little lyric, millions have sung their way through the valley of the shadow into the light of the assurance of the Eternal Presence. First, last, and always the Bible is our Book of Confession, but its aim, above all, is to bring man to that measure of responsibility which shall make him secure in freedom with full endowment as person.

4. *Process and Structure in the Internal Life*

We need now to ask in what terms the world of reality presents itself for the identification of personal problems and the reconstruction of life through their solution. Again we take a common-sense point of view by adopting a terminology which will bring our thought within the range of every man's observation. First, every object in nature, including man and his relationships with nature and his own kind, has a *structure* by which it is externally perceived as a whole. Characteristic also of all objects, selves, and persons is the fact that *within* each there is activity, release of energy or process. By these two features, we know the world. A tree has structure of cellulose, roots and branches, and also a process of photosynthesis in the leaves and the circulation of sap in the cambium layer. Every species of plant from the least to the greatest has these two properties. The atom also is an organized entity with proton and electrons in dynamic relationship.

Rise in complexity is always marked by change in structure to meet demands of process. In animals, the unit of life, the cell, is enclosed by a membrane setting it off from other cells as an individual, but it is in contact with other cells structurally related in a body with skeletal framework and metabolism in ebb and flow of building up and wearing down. The nervous system has its structure as does the brain, and in both there is the activity of electrical impulses meeting the resistance of and passing through the synapses into spreading neural paths. Mind has its structure in thoughts, ideas, and complexes, with processes of feeling and reason. Logical connection is a structure, exerting a force in communication. Language is a structure of symbols using physical elements for the processes of speech. A sentence is a structure through which an idea flows progressively into another idea in the activity of meaning. Habits are structures for repetitive performance of skills. Customs and institutions are structures for the control of human behavior. True, deeper physical and chemical analyses tend to reduce the differences between structure and process to the vanishing point since any structure ultimately appears as complicated activity. Mass and energy are one. Sir Arthur Eddington's description of his table is a case in point.[4] The table is structure but its microscopic elements, in dynamic interaction, are wide apart, more like a sponge than a solid rest for the elbow. Modern physics discloses a universe that is "alive." Certainly it is not static. Mechanism in the strict, conventional sense seems no longer tenable. At best, in whatever way we conceive it, mechanism is instrumental to process, shaping, holding it, but any attained form waits for new life in more adequate forms for fuller purposes.

---

[4] Eddington, Sir Arthur. *The Nature of the Physical World*, Introduction. New York: The Macmillan Company, 1928.

Religion, in the terms of our thought as the adventure of the self into personhood, has been subject also to the structuring of forms designed to serve it, but always with the possibility of arresting it. In the experience of Israel, it began with free movement expressed as a "going out not knowing whither," attaching itself to altars under the open sky; conceiving of covenant to establish the relationship between God and man in terms of direct intimacy. Then came the period of simple law with the free movement of the tent of the Lord from place to place, and finally the vast overgrowth of institution, rite, and ceremony, a structure for ecclesiasticism in full swing. But this, in all the glory of Solomon, passed to open the way for release of spirit again.

When Jesus came, he found religion stalemated into set forms. He proclaimed the liberation of the captives and announced a new freedom under God in his conception of the kingdom. The same was repeated in Paul, and continued to be the recurring characteristic of western religious history. Structured institution is inescapable as means, but devastating to the spirit when it cramps and attempts to fixate any stage of development. With respect to it, life ultimately becomes defiant and revolutionary. It is for this reason, if for no other, that a continuous psychotherapeutic agent must be available within the institution of organized religion to use the tensions of growth and change creatively and to direct personal experience in ampler ways. Process and structure on all levels of existence are the identifiable means by which God brings new out of the old in continuity and liberation. What this means for the renewal of the inner life we must now attempt to formulate.

In the Fourth Gospel, where the writer undertakes to interpret the meaning of Jesus to the Greek mind, there are two incidents which underscore the point we are making in this exposition of psychotherapy or the therapy of religious faith. One is the interview of Jesus with Nicodemus, the learned teacher of Israel, in whom the spirit of adventure had not been suffocated by the cult of scholarship and official responsibility. It was by night that he came, but he came. His thought of God was based upon "signs" which interrupted the ordinary course of nature or, in other ways, manifested the presence of the extraordinary. Jesus came directly to the issue—"Unless one is born anew, he cannot see the kingdom of God." This is to say, among other things, that whatever may have been the attainment of religion in Judaism, its genius could only be made secure by self-transcendence. It must be born anew.

In the second passage, the report of the Evangelist and the point which he makes is a good example of the psychotherapeutic process. The first problem which Jesus faces with the woman of Samaria, as he meets her by the well at Sychar, is the establishment of a relationship of confidence between himself and her. She approaches him in a mood of detachment, defensiveness, and resentment, formed in the prejudice of social attitudes which belonged to her group. She challenges his intrusion. She obtrudes differences of nationality to prevent a closer scrutiny of her conduct. Jesus ignores her desire for argument about the relative

virtues of Jews and Samaritans. This is not the engagement
he has with her. He seeks to find common, noncontroversial
ground in the simple need which both he and she share.
She has come to the well to draw water and he is thirsty.
There is further sharing in the reference to their common
ancestral father "who gave us the well." He makes a deferential gesture toward her. It is a natural, sincere request—
"Give me a drink." She recoils at this, and seems, for a moment, to bask in her acknowledged advantage. She has a
vessel with which to draw, and he does not. He admits the
fact, but, in her retort, he sees opportunity to make the
transition to the real business in hand.

Jesus begins to lead her from concentration upon secondary physical need to the deeper need of herself as a person.
In his metaphor of the eternal spring, he touches her at the
center and, although she is confused about his meaning for
a moment, the effect of the remark is to change her attitude
from negative to positive. Unwittingly, almost before she
knows it, she is responding to what he has to give. Her inner need is beginning to reach out for something better.
Jesus forthrightly comes to the main issue—her actual manner of life. "Go call your husband and come here." Promptly,
as though surprised at her words, she tells the truth. "I have
no husband." Jesus commends her for her honesty and enables her to look squarely at herself. "You are right . . . ;
for you have had five husbands, and he whom you now have
is not your husband." [5]

---

[5] John 4:16-18. (RSV)

The woman winces that the interview has taken such a turn. She acknowledges his perception of the facts about her, but seeks refuge in a controversy of another kind than that arising from differences of nationality. She knows the trick of hiding behind generalizations, especially those high-sounding ones sometimes used in theological discussion. She wants to compare places of worship and get Jesus going on the merits of Jerusalem versus Mt. Gerizim. But he will have none of this. He cuts right through to the main point where again both he and she stand together. Neither in this mountain nor in Jerusalem, but "in spirit and *in truth*" alone God is worshiped. This is person-to-person talk; person-to-person facing of the God of persons. In her truth-telling, she opens the eternal spring of the inner life; she worships by the well, symbol of replenishment under God wherever one is in his need. The renewal that comes when old structures of fixed attitudes, hates, prejudices, and rationalizations give way to the process of truth is explicit in the words, "She left her water jar," and went into the city telling everybody, "Come, see a man who told me all things that ever I did." Actually, Jesus does not do that in so many words even though it is the main purpose of the writer to show that he "knew what was in man." He does something far better. He enables her to tell him, to confess, to clear her mind, and start again with a new-found joy of adventure and wholeness she had not known before. This is the kind of renovation continually needed from childhood to old age if the internal life is to be kept resilient, growing, and abounding in zest for living.

In Paul, the issue is the same, though the case which he makes for it is somewhat different. The conflict is none the less inward and none the less under necessity to find resolution through facing the truth. The structure in which Paul is confined and under which he chafes is described in various ways as "law," the Mosaic and rabbinical law defining precisely how one could attain righteousness. He refers also to the "law of his members," the flesh taking the field and warring against the "law in his mind" so that "when he would do good," evil threatens or takes over. He feels susceptible in his best moments to impulses that divert him from his chosen purpose. There is no hope of rescue in the law, for it only accentuates, as structure always does, the very difficulties with which one wrestles. Repressive "Thou shalt nots" are not the strategy for outwitting the power of the instincts as Jesus so clearly set forth in the Sermon on the Mount.

We see in Paul a restive, dynamic nature, intent on attainment of perfectionist righteousness, and getting in his own way with every effort he made. Then the day comes when the old structure is shattered because it can no longer hold together the elements that are struggling within him. It is a conflict between the self and the person in Paul, the former deriving its character from the older order of his fathers and intellectualized by a rabbinical education, the latter the thrust of freedom toward fuller life demanding the process of faith and grace. Once this insight is gained, the mind reworks the ground of the older self until it is transformed (Romans 1-8) and eventually superseded in "no longer I, but Christ." It is this process that we have in mind when we speak of religion and psychotherapy—"the art and the theory of the internal life of man."

5. *Grace and the Seven Steps*

Can we now set the elements of the process in some ordered form which will serve as guide in practicing the art of nurturing growth in personhood? We shall attempt it by turning to some old words often glibly pronounced, but which, when seen in the full context of the inner life, hold the main secret of man's adventure.

Anyone reflecting for a moment on his position in the world will be almost overwhelmed by the perception of the wealth of unearned favor in the midst of which he lives and without which his existence would be impossible. The air we breathe, the light that floods our day, the warmth that accompanies it, the electromagnetic forces which hold us to the spinning earth, the extravagance of nature's resources for the support of life, the integrated arrangement for our birth, the intricate structure and functioning of the human body, the social influences that shape us from infancy to adulthood, are bare items in a cosmos of complex objects and relations. By our own acts as individuals, we did absolutely nothing in making all this provision for our coming and our nurture.

Indeed, if one could take an honest inventory of everything one does from birth to old age, he would be unable to find a single occasion in which he and he alone acted without the collaboration of an incalculable host of visible and invisible forces. To labor the obvious, consider the body. Think of the man whose heart in autopsy revealed a half dozen scars, each marking a crisis of which he was completely unaware until the last one took him. Years had been given to him without conscious effort on his part, and he died without knowing anything about this work of an unseen providence. Think of the immunities we acquire automatically—the battle in the blood every hour against infection, the magic of hormones, the balance in metabolism, and so on. Time would fail to mention even a good fraction of all that sustains us each day that we live. In all our talk about freedom, do we ever think that even the word would not exist if we did not have millions of slaves working for us every minute of our lives? The universe is ours without asking for it. But surely we have this possession for a purpose. For what man can make of man? If so, then what amazing capital with which to start!

All this unearned favor is in itself enough to banish any thought that the world is against us or that we can let ourselves off easy in any situation. But when we add to this natural grace, the grace of God in Jesus Christ, touching us at the crucial point of the redemption of self in fulfilled personhood, the soul leaps for joy in the richness of amazing love and the prospect of unmeasured spiritual opportunity. This substantial fact of man's acceptance by God is the ground and guarantee of Christian psychotherapy. What it means when applied to the conditions of the internal life we shall discuss as the way of the seven steps.

First, one must face himself as he is. This calls for *confession*.[6] Basically, the word refers to the method by which the content of the self as internalized past experience is brought under the deliberate and conscious scrutiny of the person as he responds to life as a whole under God. In the New Testament, the term means, literally, bringing to the outside what is inside; uncovering that which is concealed; inspecting the sources of difficulty and inadequacy; ventilating and clarifying attitudes and feelings by verbalizing them. This process, in some form, is indispensable to what is sometimes called self-acceptance, but it should be understood that this is not an end in itself, certainly not satisfaction with all that one finds in oneself.

Rather confession is telling the truth about ourselves, facing our rationalizations, trying to understand the root of the feelings that sometimes surge through us without our knowing why. It is penetrating the sources of anxiety and laying them out in the presence of Another who sees with us and "in whom we live and move and have our being" as persons. The value of confession of this sort is often enhanced by sharing one's "troubles" with a trusted person who has competence in religion and can act as guide, who will understand rather than judge, and leave to the individual and to God the final appraisal of thoughts and acts. Confession of this sort is not something done once and for all, although there are occasions when it is especially necessary in getting a fresh start. Nothing is more stifling, more

---

[6] *The Best in Pastoral Psychology*, Edited by Simon Doniger, p. 96f. Great Neck: Pastoral Psychology Press, 1952.

arresting of the adventure of living than the settled attitude that one has done his "confessing" and is now "all right" for all future time. This is that self-righteousness which fixates a person, and which, as Jesus said in his reference to certain attitudes of the Pharisees, must be "exceeded."

It should be emphasized that confession must be accurate if it is to be helpful. One must not morbidly blame himself, indulge in self-accusation that has no ground in fact. One must accept, love himself realistically for everything he can approve and respect in his life. It is no sin to credit ourselves with what is our due. Indeed, it is sin not to do so. What is explicitly there in the "record" should be acknowledged even though we may not wish to advertise our virtues. There is no finer humility than accuracy, and this is a rare art when it comes to understanding ourselves and thereby entering into honest relations with God and our fellow men.

Furthermore, confession must be specific, dealing with concrete and actual situations in our lives which we wish to transcend. One can always say that he is a "sinner," but unless he can say specifically "wherein," confession becomes mere form. The fault that is cloaked in generalization and cannot be identified for what it really is cannot be corrected. The chronic confessor, who enjoys his "sins" by vague reference to them to give an impression of humility, is an addict nursing a truncated or dwarfed personhood. Confessions made in corporate settings have their value but in the nature of the case employ generalities which do not as a rule present to the mind the source of difficulty. Such a statement as "We have done those things which we ought not to have done and left undone those things which we ought to have done" covers everything and touches nothing in particular.

One aspect of confession, a kind of background factor much discussed in the literature of today, is guilt. We need make only a passing reference to it, for it has been over-worked by some writers. Proper perspective on New Testament teaching, regarding the basic significance of guilt in the dynamics of religious experience, can be rather simply stated. Guilt is the emotional reaction to an act which an individual judges to be a violation of his standards of thought and conduct. In its healthy form, it is the recognition of the gap between goal and accomplishment and becomes the incentive for further improvement. A sinful act in biblical usage separates man from God, an act which, in our perspective, causes the self to "miss the mark" of personhood.[7] In mental disease guilt may take on a morbid

---

[7] Biblical thought also relates sin to disease as cause and effect. The question of the disciples, in the case of the man born blind (John 9:2), "Who sinned, this man or his parents?" makes the point. Modern medicine, however, views disease as a condition which has its own etiology and which, in its organic character, lies outside the deliberate choice of the individual. This outlook now prevails so widely that one would rarely think of "sin" as the cause of cancer, tuberculosis, malaria, or any other disease whose source is known to be beyond the reach of the will of the patient. But when we come to illnesses of the functional type, especially mental disorders, the question enters another frame of reference which includes social influences affecting the personality. Jesus and Paul warned against anxiety. Today excessive or long-continued anxiety states are known causes of disease. Is anxiety sin? Is the "sin" of parents the cause of delinquency among "teen-agers"? To put the question another way, in what degree may acts commonly called "sinful" be translated into the categories of disease? This is an area for fruitful conversation between theologians and physicians.

character due to etiological factors in the early development of a personality. Certain types of religious influence may reinforce these factors and fixate them, but the basic distortion stems from social experience structured in the self rather than from religion as such. The kind of religion that is mainly a defense against the instincts, instead of the transformation of them, lends itself more readily to reinforcement of morbid character. Such guilt must be treated as a part of disease by specialized forms of psychotherapy which supplement the normal resources of religion.[8] It is worth noting here, however, that even in Paul's conception of sin as a kind of personal principle in the world, there is immediate remedy in abounding grace which need leave no one under oppressive burden of guilt. But more of that later. For the present, the word of the psalmist, "Behold, thou desirest truth in the inward parts" will suffice for confession.

Closely allied to confession in Christian psychotherapy is *repentance*. The word means resolute change, renovation of mind and purpose, conversion. In sequence with confession, it is the elimination of what one has discovered to be restricting, limiting him in the joy of advancing personhood. If confession should be likened to a certain kind of surgery, or a catharsis eliminating disease processes in the body, repentance would be building up an immunity to

---

[8] One of the most significant signs of the times is the new spirit of collaboration which is developing among clergymen and psychiatrists. The prospect for the future, as this movement grows, is most inviting. Indeed, it may mark the beginning of a new day in religion and medicine.

prevent the recurrence of the trouble. It is having done with what one judges to be negatively related to the good life. It is internal health of spirit motivating a different kind of external behavior. The kingdom of increased competency for living is always at hand for those who are ready to change their minds by eradicating obsolete and outgrown attitudes which hamper growth in maturity. One matter in connection with both confession and repentance that must be stressed, especially for the Protestant, is the acceptance of responsibility for oneself, readiness to take initiative in availing oneself of the resources of religion. Hans Schaer has rightly pointed out that the Protestant must bear the burden of his own unconscious inasmuch as he cannot accept dependency on a church which does all important things for him sacramentally by simple submission to its authority.[9]

For some, this responsibility for themselves is too great in their own strength. Nevertheless, in the Protestant faith where the emphasis is placed on what the individual does, there are abundant means for undergirding and freeing life for all who will properly seek them and use them in a thoroughgoing, intelligent fashion. Repentance, then, is decisive action with respect to habits and attitudes that obstruct advance in wholesome, happy living. With confession it is the cleansing of the inner life.

In this exposition of Christian psychotherapy, we are attempting to keep our concepts as closely related as pos-

---

[9] Schaer, Hans, *Religion and the Cure of Souls in Jung's Psychology*, p. 179. New York: Pantheon Books, Inc., 1950.

sible to the actual dynamics of human living as every man knows them. Our view of confession and repentance goes deeper than the formal transactions so often associated with them in the conventions of religious practice. Settings and occasions for their use are necessary and, in some degree, must be formalized, but it is always in connection with the internal crisis for growth in personhood that they do their real work. Apart from that, they are words without important consequence. In the same way, we must think of *forgiveness,* the third step in the religious process which we are expounding. To make clear our meaning here, perhaps we ought first to divest our thought of certain naive conceptions of forgiveness. In the first place, it is not merely "getting off" from or avoiding the consequences of our acts. We do "get off," and we do go on living in spite of many of our errors. But to think of forgiveness as escape, or a condoning of mistakes by an "Oh, forget it!" is to treat a matter of great importance in a superficial, not to say, a frivolous manner. Life is not reversible. There can be no acts without consequences in a universe where, we are told, the lifting of an arm produces a disturbance in the sun.

The essence of forgiveness is that no man need be bound by any past event of his life even though that event cannot be eradicated as a fact. This means that a past act may cease to have effect upon one's further adventure as earlier experiences of the self are reassimilated and tranformed in the new experiences of the person. This does not imply that forgiveness is a right. It is a gift intensifying opportunity for undertaking a reconstruction of the self. It removes the

sense of guilt in the service of the freedom needed for
the reconstruction. On any other ground than effectualizing
a redemptive event in the internal life, forgiveness is a
sham and an offense. It cannot accomplish its purpose except as confession and repentance are related to it and
dynamically complete it. "Forgive us our trespasses as we
forgive those who trespass against us" is predicated plainly
on the assumption that the self is involved in relations
with others, rightness with whom is the condition of acceptance before God as a person.

Jesus' refusal to give a mechanical rule regarding forgiveness, with the implication of a continuously forgiving
attitude, reflects the need for balance in internalized social
experience and acknowledges the actual state of social relations among imperfect human beings. The reconciliation
of conflicting elements in the self by which resentments,
anxieties, prejudice, are transmuted through love, is the
condition of that self-transcendence which is reconciliation
with God. In Christ, God's grace for this reconciliation is
manifest. The regeneration of the social order waits upon
this change in the internal life under the leadership of a
religion whose art and theory we are just beginning to
understand.

But when all this is said, there remains the fact that no
internal change can be permanent or implement further
change until it expresses itself in an appropriate act. Christian psychotherapy, therefore, involves *obedience*. This, we
hasten to add, does not mean subservience to an arbitrary
authority or conformity to creedal and ecclesiastical de-

mand for their own sake. These are structures which are useful but, in extreme forms, can also be obstructive. By obedience, we mean response to *insight*, acting in accordance with the new light and the new strength that has come through confession, repentance, and forgiveness. This is the inward "law," bringing together into new relationship hitherto opposing and restrictive forces within the self. Obedience is the exercise of freedom in the choice of those actions, including communication, that are the outward sign of the inward regenerative power of grace. The function of obedience is thus twofold: It acts reflexively upon the individual, confirming his advance into personhood, and it contributes to change in social relations.

To all these terms, describing inward transaction with reality, we now add *faith* and *joy*. We have intimated that all men, in a very real sense, live under grace whether they walk consciously in the Christian way or not. It is equally true that all men live by faith, that is, by outreach for the better possibility presently before them, even though their perception of the goal may not accord with good judgment or religious standard. For biblical man, however, faith is the vital breath of the human adventure, reckoned in the beginning as righteousness, restated as the "substance of things hoped for," and continuing as the means of keeping contact with eternal spirit in the mastery of changing times and circumstances. Faith is relying on "that which is permanent in the nature of things."

In the New Testament, joy is the word invented to describe the health of the Christian mind in offering antidote for the enervating pleasures of the Graeco-Roman age. It stands at the opposite of the scale from gratification, satiety, and dull despair. It is not ecstasy, not elation, not animal euphoria. It is the emotional accompaniment of the total response of the human organism to the higher possibilities of being and becoming. It is the synthesis of all desire in overarching purpose; the zest for living; the vigor of maturity in full stride. It is the inward unity which brings dynamic peace in the midst of conflict sustained by the certainty that ultimately God works all things together for good, including the good that we shall never see. It is the energy that makes us equal to the final challenge of our goal in the race for personhood. Joy is creative living by the power of the Spirit wherever we are, the inward sign of health which the world cannot give or take away.

Finally, special mention must be made of the community of believers which surrounds the individual and brings him the support of relations with others who jointly are engaged in the activities of religious living. The anxieties which arise from solitariness are assuaged by the intimacies of this association in understanding love and by the reassurance of shared meanings deeply rooted in a long past with God at the center of devotion and service. Let it be emphasized, however, that Christian psychotherapy demands the acceptance of the individual in the integrity of his uniqueness without pressure of conformity to group stereotype, without bondage to practices alien to his inward character, and without reference to previous conditions of conduct.

This is the heart of Christian love. In this perspective, the church is not an association of selves *which* enjoy the conviviality of sanctified fraternity. It is a community of growing persons *who* have the right to protection from the aggression of an imposed structure of fixed belief and the need for the freedom to seek fulfillment through direct responsiveness to God. There is no other way by which a self can become fully a person. Without this freedom, religion confuses security with boredom, puts on the vestment of pretension, and stifles the impulse toward variation and creativity.

Had Jesus chosen to limit his activity to what was safe for him as a self, he would have continued his work as a carpenter, conformed to a formal Judaism, and lost his identity in the subjugated masses of the Roman Empire. The measure of his personhood is the resistance which he offered to overwhelming worldly power and a suffocating legalism. This was the act of renunciation from which he "returned in the power of the Spirit," at one with God, to become the Lord and Master of all who search for divine companionship beyond the bounds of group-enforced creed. Any society can produce a self; ultimately, only God, using self, can create a person.

In all this, we are emphasizing two important aspects of Christian psychotherapy. First, as we have intimated previously, conflict in any life situation is rooted in the history of the self and is resolved by a recapitulation or reliving of that history. By this process, the structure of the self is altered, the past is reassimilated and transcended. Second, the internal agent of this activity is the person as constituted by those meanings and values which are related to his ultimate goal as a child of God. The scene of this inward transaction, "so far as that depends on the man himself," is marked by the kind of reflection, meditation, and prayer which belong to the experience of worship and which prepare the way for recovery, for a new feeling of wholeness, and a more ordered sense of responsible action. On this, we shall have more to say in the next chapter.

Meanwhile, it must be noted that the need for a more intelligent and disciplined use of religion grows apace in our world. The plague of mankind in our time is the impersonal drive to suppress the individual in the interest of a deadening social process endowed with the glamor of subtle appeal to altruistic sentiment. Even the great axiom that life is found by losing it suffers perversion at the hands of those who serve this cause. The self, affiliated with this process, may seduce the emerging person in every heart and may at last, if not redeemed, reduce free men to automatons and robots. This is the illness which threatens to become epidemic. The church and its ministries are called to stand guard over the children of God lest they fall victim to the disease of drift and contentment with static and materialistic valuations of life. With devotion and skill, the curative power of faith, sustained by the blessed community of freedom and love, must be made available for every man's adventure in enduring the pain of that new birth by which self is transformed into Christ-like personhood.

9. THE WORK OF GOD

1. *God and Time*

KOHELETH, WHOSE WORDS ARE CONTAINED in Ecclesiastes, announces a theory of time in formulating his view of the problem of man. He states that he has "seen everything that is done under the sun," that "for everything there is a season," that what "is, already has been," and that what "will be, already has been." The note of skepticism which arises from this endless cycle of repetition is due, however, to the mystery of the hidden purpose of existence. There is some consolation in the fact that the "business" given to the "sons of men" is "from God" who "has made everything beautiful" or fitting "in its time." But God has also "put eternity into man's mind," and then so hedged him in "that he cannot find what God has done from the beginning." It is man's despair that with this capacity for "eternity," he cannot live in the dimension of it. He must be content "to be happy and enjoy" himself with "eating and drinking" and being "busy." To strive for goals beyond these is "vanity."

Modern physics and metaphysics have taken a hand in stating the case for time. Eddington writes about "pointer readings" on a space-time continuum.[1] Einstein contrasts a one-dimensional continuum with a two-dimensional plane and a three-dimensional object. He then notes that a fourth factor, time, enters all calculations of motion with decisive effects.[2] Whitehead speaks of the future being "immanent" in the present, of the passage from "re-enaction to anticipation" through intermediate stages of "transition".[3] In this view, time appears to be fluid, moving like a stream in which concrete occasions are islands set off from one another in a relational order or sequence. Our own version of this has been previously expressed in terms of recapitulation and transcendence. We shall continue in this form of thought, but we should mark some of the words of Koheleth. "I know," he says, "that whatever God does endures forever; nothing can be added to it, nor anything taken from it; God hath made it so." (Ecclesiastes 3:14 RSV)

In our common-sense experience, everyone has a feeling for time and, on a little reflection, can recognize its decisive importance in all human affairs. We speak of a past, a present, and a future, a kind of spacing of events in our thought as though to suggest that time is perceived only by separating them from one another, by saying that such

---

[1] *The Nature of the Physical World*, p. 253.

[2] *The Evolution of Physics*, pp. 219-20.

[3] *Adventures of Ideas*, p. 248f. New York: The Macmillan Company, 1937.

and such happened so many years ago or only yesterday; when the first baby was born, or when a loved one died. We have mechanical devices, calendars and clocks, for regulating our lives but, apart from these, time always seems attached to some substance—a place, objects, people, or a date that stands for a complex situation such as July 4, 1776.

In recollections from our studies of history and from personal experience, images and symbols in memory *place* events in a certain order or series. They stand apart in measures of distance that vary, so that we can distinguish "long ago" from last week and today. If we pause long enough to examine what we recall, many objects and persons will come before our minds, and they will appear as we observed them directly or perceived them as reported by another. Yet all these elements hold together *now* in this present, and from them we project plans for the future, the substance of things we shall do then, abstractly conceived. But with respect to these, we have to *wait* for time. We cannot bring tomorrow's events into today, or evening into morning. We can change a plan for tomorrow and carry it out today as we can speed up our travel, but all this is our adaptation to time, and never in the least affects time itself. Nothing is more real than time, yet it is so elusive that the best we can do is to translate it into spatial terms as so much ground covered or so much work done in an hour. Time, we say, is the stuff of life, so important in fact, that we often talk about "saving" it, knowing that we are speaking in a figure, for it can neither be saved nor expended. We can only change our relation to it in a certain space setting and judge results by saying such things as, "Look, I *did all this* in an hour!" We can call the hour ours only by what we did in it. The hour itself is not "there." We know time best in heart throbs, measuring our relations with it until at last it settles everything for us. We say it is "running out" on us, but actually, it is we who run out, leaving it unaffected and only what we did in it spatially as the record of our passing through it.[4] And each of us knows time in his own way as Thomas Mann, in a lucid passage of *Joseph in Egypt,* remarks that every man is the center of the world, drawing all impressions of it into himself and sending forth such responses as he can.

An artist seated by his easel at the roadside looks out toward the landscape which he has decided to paint. In the foreground, there is a tall tree on the edge of a lake. Beyond, the waves rippling quietly toward the farther shore toss up and down a little boat with a sail. Farther still on the rising ground are rows of trees threaded between open fields, and from these, the eye moves upward where the blue mountain touches fleecy clouds in the sky. We watch the transfer of this scene to the canvas as the artist's hand moves back and forth from his palette, mixing the colors to match what his eye catches on tree, water, and hill. When his

---

[4] The inscription on Lorado Taft's statue of "Time" in Chicago reads:

"Time goes, you say? Ah, no.
Alas! Time stays. We go.

work is done, we see the landscape just as it looked in nature, but it is on a flat surface with length and breadth. That, however, presents no problem, for our minds, aided by stereoscopic vision, at once supply the third dimension of depth just as the artist saw it and set all the features of the scene in perspective. Yet, unless we are unusually perceptive, we shall miss the determining factor in that scene. Rating the artist's skill as high as we choose, we know that it came by time and, if this is his masterpiece, that, too, is a monument to time.

And this is not all; far from it. The picture will be different if the artist does his work at sunrise, at midmorning, at noon, afternoon, or at sunset. The lights and shadows changing with the spinning earth will require another mixture of colors. If he comes in spring, the leaves on the tree will be a bright, young green, and the fields freshly turned by the plow. If he comes at midsummer, the grain will be golden, ready for harvest. In autumn, all the colors of the rainbow will gather in gorgeous festival of protest against death, and later yield to winter's white crystals blanketing valley and hill in sleep. Finally, we know that had the artist come a hundred thousand years ago, he would have taken away on his canvas a glacier glistening in the sun instead of the scene we have described. Change the scene as we will to any part of the globe, and time will stand in the midst as invisible monitor of all we survey.

If anything is constant as context within which all spatial relativity appears, it is time. It is the matrix of events, pervading and conditioning all energy-substance but con-

ditioned by none. It is anthropism, of course, but more
than myth that at New Year's, we speak of Father Time,
and more than poetic fancy that led Browning, reflecting
a phrase from Psalm 31, to say,

> Our times are in his hand. . . .

And now perhaps we are ready to feel the impact of our
earlier journey through the Bible. We spoke of the soul
of Israel as that inner unity of all the diverse experiences
recorded there, the ebb and flow of the internal life in engagement with successive occasions, each recapitulating
what went before and seeking to transcend it. We felt the
sweep of time through periods of pasts entering into presents and becoming futures in ceaseless change. The modern
physicist needs his light years, and the geologist contrives
figures of many ciphers to express magnitudes of time and
space that leave the average of us gasping but unperceiving.
It is enough for the Bible to say, "In the beginning," a
phrase as empty and as full of time as a million light years.
It might just as well have been "Once upon a time," and,
for the purpose in hand, just as useful. The story must start
and inevitably pays tribute to time.

From that point on, the adventure of life in man as person is spread out as upon a canvas with all scenes painted
in, the land and the people in bright colors of hope and
courage, and the darker shades of discouragement and
failure. We feel drawn into the picture, for the more we
look and understand, the more we sense that we are in it
too. The external scene of our life is vastly different, but

the internal issue remains the same—what man can make of man under God through His agent, time. For all the stark realism that marks its pages, the Bible knows no final cynicism, no ultimate failure, no dead end. It lays out the thoroughfare of the soul beginning with self-affirmation and moving on to transfigured personhood in Jesus Christ, who came in the "fullness of time," and who, when lifted up, draws all men unto himself in the unfolding possibilities of their own time. This is the work of God. This is his appointment with us here and now.

2. *Separation and Reconciliation*

Each man must seize his opportunity where he stands within the bounds set for his adventure and with such powers as he has at his disposal. This is the fact of his solitariness. He moves in a great company. Yet he walks alone. By the act of his creation, he was separated from his Creator with freedom in this separation as his basic attribute and the source of his anxiety. This presents the problem which all religions have sought to solve. The Judeo-Christian tradition, explicit in the Bible, affirms that the solution comes by the free act of binding life back into its source in God and going on to responsibility in a maturity equal to the risks of changing settings and circumstances. The relevance and the appeal of this view are found in its articulation of experience native to every individual. Birth is a separation of great consequence. Some speak of it as a trauma. Ferenzci, a Hungarian physician,

who practiced in Vienna, described the state of the living
foetus before birth as "unconditioned omnipotence." He
might have called it omnipotent dependency or that state
of effortlessness not even involving breathing or digestion
where, in fact, there is no gap between need and satisfaction, no desire. Regardless of terms, birth is a crisis initiat-
ing a situation of anxiety as the neuromuscular organism
seeks satisfaction of its needs from the environment.

The human infant, for all its potentiality, is among the
most helpless of living creatures. The culture to which it
immediately becomes subject in humanizing it imposes delays in meeting its needs. It is plastic and responsive in its
adaptation to external conditions, but gaps between hunger
and feeding are unavoidable. Sex, already active at birth
by virtue of nature's provision for posterity, becomes im-
perious in its demands at puberty. Society, however, de-
crees delays until the individual is deemed competent and
responsible, and prescribes the steps by which he may ac-
ceptably exercise the function of sex. The intervals between need and satisfaction give rise to desire, and the
greater the discrepancy between the two, the greater the
demand for substitution and sublimation. Training can
do much to assuage and direct desire to keep it within
cultural bounds, but the tensions of delay are inevitable.
All this arises from the imperative of life that the child
shall make his way as a separated individual. At the age of
self-consciousness, his awareness of this condition is a decisive factor in his development as a self and a person. He
must progressively take charge of himself and finally,

through adolescence, emancipate himself from the dependencies of childhood. The importance of love in the experience of the child, enabling him to make the transitions by giving him support and a sense of belonging, along with the perils of his inward fears of rejection, is a favorite theme among psychologists. The main principle is an old one in religion, although new knowledge has made the meaning of love more precise and suggested better ways of understanding and ministering to people in their loneliness and anxieties.

Among illustrations of these, none in all religious literature is more realistic and poignant than the case of Job in the Old Testament. It is a masterpiece, both from the standpoint of its surpassing literary quality and the depth of its penetration into the anguish that accompanies full awareness of extreme affliction. Job's sense of isolation is complete. The "friends" who argue with him represent his own inward attempt, with the best wisdom available, to think his way out of the bewilderment that follows sudden catastrophic misfortune ultimately affecting him most acutely at the very center of his being. One by one, all known human explanations for such events are cast aside as inadequate. At last, he issues a straight challenge to God Himself. His complaints and accusations are directed against the fundamental order of things which allows injustice to destroy the work of a man's hands, disease to rot his body and, at last, to treat his soul as nothing. All the questions raised here are common properties of the human heart, compounded in a crisis of utter separation.

There are no verbal terms in which the resolution of the problem can be set. The grand panoramic vision of the universe succeeds in humbling Job by forcing him to swallow his words in sackcloth and ashes. Orion and the Pleiades, leviathan in the great deep, reduce him to physical size. They speak not to his dignity as man with capacity to perceive these things and reason about them. Perspective on one's condition by viewing it in a system of larger relationships assuages the pain through giving the mind something with which to divert itself from overoccupation with morbid thoughts and self-pity, but there is no satisfying *intellectual* answer to the problem of suffering.

In the last analysis, there is only one way to get the answer to tragedy and that is *to live through it,* to endure the reality of it with fortitude and faith, and use the experience as a way of more deeply knowing oneself by internally transmuting the pain, the resentments, the anger, into nobler spirit. In this undertaking, God ceases to be enemy and becomes companion. He closes the gap of separation in the newly found peace of the transformed self-acceptance of personhood. As such, the struggle becomes a triumph in life's adventure. In this, as in the broader issues on the world scene, time imposes the requirements for change in a proper conjunction of events. The people of Israel knew the bitterness and destruction of war, and their prophets dreamed of a warless world, a way of so relating nations that their separation would at least stop short of violent attack, but only in modern times, when communication and transportation have made of all nations one world, and when weapons have attained unparalleled firing power, have men become convinced that no war can now be won by anybody, and that to act on the basis of old assumptions is to invite mutual self-destruction. That is at least one lesson taught, at colossal cost, by the twentieth century. The ultimate fact is that man wins as *man* or not at all.

The deeper meanings of this separation as a universal aspect of human existence, supplemented by the observation that the basic unit in all nature is a structured individual, are unfolded in the central themes of the Bible. It appears in Israel as self-consciousness developing the concept of a chosen people. It is a major characteristic of the outlook of the great individuals, the prophets of the latter years. The missions of Jesus, Paul, and the leaders of succeeding centuries declare it. Indeed, human greatness is measured by the manner in which the individual solves the problem of his separation. But nowhere is the full story so plainly told as in the parables of the lost in Luke 15. The sheep that wanders away from the flock stands under threat of losing its "sheephood." The coin that is lost has no part in the beauty of the necklace to which it belonged, or no value outside of some relation with commodities in exchange. It is in the story of the two sons, however, that the heart of the gospel is disclosed in terms that are unforgettable. We scarcely need more than is stated there in less than 500 simple words. We should look at the record for a moment.

When the younger son asked for his inheritance, the

father hesitated not one moment. He gave it. When the son started away, the father said not one word about where he should go. This is just the way the human situation is, Jesus seems to say. The son, as a separated individual, is free to use the resources that belong to him and to choose his own way of using them. God, like the father, takes the risks of the freedom which could not be avoided in man as a separated creature. It is, in fact, a part of God's greatness that He can tolerate all the possibilities of evil which may grow out of the exercise of man's freedom in an eternity of time. This is the measure of His wisdom and His love. The son takes his fullest liberty. He goes into a "far country," throws restraint to the winds, indulges every desire of the flesh, until his "substance" is gone. This is one way of taking freedom. The extremity and loathsomeness of his condition at the end is suggested by his reduction to the provender of the pigs as the means of bare sustenance of physical life. This is the utmost of separation a man can know. This is what is meant by sin—deliberate choices which widen the gap between a man and his personhood in God.

At the heart of the story, it is Jesus' purpose to disclose the character of God. It is clear that God will do nothing to rob man of the freedom He has given him. He will not, like the shepherd, go after him, or, like the woman, search for him. The issue rests upon the son's initiative. He must come to himself, perceive the difference between being mere animal and a real man, and act to enter into those relations by which manhood is sustained. *He must do this much himself.* When, in repentance and humility, he acts saying, "I will arise and go," it is then that the measure of divine grace is seen, and love is manifest in all the extravagance of the reception accorded to the son. Forgiveness follows, and the restoration is complete. The sin of the older son represents another kind of separation. He was angry and "would not go in." Pride and self-righteous complacency cut him off from his brother whom he would not forgive. The father's love was nevertheless equally manifest toward him in the privilege of favor and position. We do not miss the point of Jesus' immediate intention in dealing with self-righteousness, but his disclosure of the work of God in a love that heals relationships broken by the wrong use of freedom is unmistakable.

3. *God and Community*

Thus far in considering the work of God, attention has been centered mainly on His concern for the individual. That emphasis continues to be primary, but it remains for us to examine the divine activity in the wider settings of human relations as they affect and are affected by the work of God in the individual. Earlier we mentioned the six major institutions or orders of activity by which men pursue objectives related mainly to specific and limited purposes and through which, in severally serving themselves as individuals, they also contribute to the satisfaction of human needs in general. We now wish to examine the motivation for these activities in terms of the kinds of *value* which sustain incentive in the affairs of daily life. We seek an understanding of the normative aspects of human nature in a more explicit reading of the facts than has been possible in our previous discussion, although, as in all human thought about man, some feeling for value is inevitable.

Industry is the word for all those activities of production, distribution or exchange, and consumption by which economic needs of the people are satisfied. These needs have a wide range from those required for bare subsistence to those of an expanded luxury satisfying mainly prestige and power. The basic characteristic here is that all members of a society, even dependents who are consumers only, are engaged in some degree in activity of an economic character, and are motivated by the value of exchange of goods and services whose symbol is money. This value regulates all economic undertaking, and enters into the motivations of every individual.

Government, or the state, in all its forms stands for those indispensable activities of civilized society related to the maintenance of order, the administration of justice, the common defense, and the general welfare. Although these activities have important economic aspects, the value which motivates them in their normal form is derived from the political theory of the people involved. In democracy, for example, liberty is a value for which we are willing to expend enormous economic resources. Justice, order, welfare, likewise stand for values in the common life to which every good citizen subscribes as a matter of course. In each of these functions of government, there are standards by which one judges better and worse and assigns responsibility to those whose vocation it is to serve in these capacities.

In *education,* the schools and colleges, in some respects the greatest enterprise of a democracy, we also have activities controlled by the value of skills in contributing to the productivity of the individual citizen, the conservation and transmission of knowledge, and the search for truth. The values motivating education as an undertaking of a society are both utilitarian and intrinsic.

The *professional arts*—medicine, law, teaching, and so on—partake of their own kind of value, although they are not unrelated to those already mentioned when viewed from the standpoint of a society and related specifically to human good. Health is a value served by the physician as the teacher serves education, and the lawyer justice. In the fine arts, the value relates to esthetics, the finer appreciations of the human spirit, the response to all that goes under the name of beauty and its correlates.

The *family* is the institution of primary relationships. In our culture, it is increasingly restricted to the production and nurture of new human beings. The value here is the person. Marriage is the arrangement by which men and women attain mutual fulfillment through a union of sexual love that advances to mature responsibility for children. The family, above all, is the place where conscience emerges to guide the self in its relations with other selves, and where the work of God, in sovereign purpose, begins to direct the person by reason and love.

The family also renders important service to citizenship. American culture, in its political and social functioning, has its theory centering in the rights of the individual. And yet democracy cannot work effectively unless it is a part of the internal equipment of every citizen. It must be an *experience* dynamically organized in attitude, habit, and ideals. As such, it derives its character basically from the interactions of family living. The rudiments of justice are learned in the adjudication of differences and the adjustment of rivalries in the nursery. Security, acceptance of authority, the claim to freedom, and the capacity to discern the relevance of each in determining behavior appropriate to occasion are crucial elements in the rearing and education of children. Likewise responsibility, which begins with the self-control acquired in the care of the body and such elementary acts as putting toys away without being told, is rooted in the home and moves through the widening circles of school and playground to high affairs of state. The cabin on the frontier is inseparable from the White House where Lincoln, as a free and competent *person*, presided over the crisis of a house divided against *itself*.

Most acute among all relations in our society is the conflict of secular values with the family, the most sensitive of all social organisms. It is the place where all other interests seek to take their profit and expand their undertakings by the responses there to a maximum degree. The family is the ultimate market for everything that the community produces. It is here that the crisis for personhood stands forth in clearest light and calls for resources which will enable the home to resist encroachments that threaten its integrity and interfere with its task. The democratic state, recognizing the social value of the family and aware of the perils which it faces, has done much to provide protective measures and, through education, to assist it constructively to solve its problems. Effective use of this assistance, however, depends upon the capacity of parents to see clearly where the issue lies and to maintain a sense of responsibility in their relations with their children. The main fact is that no law or other measure can prescribe a technique to govern the interaction of parents and children. Love, the great enzyme of life, cannot be compelled and, if it could be, it would cease to be love, lacking the free spontaneity of concern for others for their own sake which is love's most important ingredient. Love can only be learned and lived. It is for this reason, a reason derived from the actual dynamics of living in community, that religion, whose organized expression is the church, is more closely related to the family than to any other institution. The family and the church are one in their concern for persons as ends in themselves. This is the purpose that justifies and fulfills all other human purposes.[5]

---

[5] It is pertinent to note here the place of family experience in shaping religious attitudes and beliefs. The predominant influence flows from the bisexuality of the individual in his own constitution and his continuous exposure socially to both sexes. The ancients openly acknowledged this by providing gods and goddesses in their pantheons.

Certain generalizations may now be made concerning these institutions or organized activities. First, all members of the society are dependent upon them for the satisfaction of specified needs and are indirectly involved in all of them. Second, within the community there is a division of labor whereby individuals engage in one or more sets of activities to serve the interests of others who are otherwise occupied. Third, each of these institutions, including the persons involved, is directed toward a specific objective, the thing society expects it to do, and each tends to pursue its aims without reference to the work for which others are responsible. This results in concentration upon a particular

---

In Hebrew experience the role of the female was absorbed by the role of the male. Monotheism with emphasis on the transcendence of God was a natural consequence. In modern religious thought, bisexuality, divested of organic elements, appears in the attempt to reconcile the transcendence of God (male aspects) with the immanence of God (female aspects). Emphasis on one or the other, or the integration of both, expresses a thinker's reaction to family life. In those cultures and individual families which are strongly patriarchal the tendency is in the direction of transcendence, even to the point of the Wholly Other. On the other hand, pure humanism takes the opposite direction. All these elements can be identified in the predilections of a thinker as they manifest themselves in the way he assimilates religious thought of the past and reacts to the current reality situation. Likewise the use of the paradoxical form of thought and the idealization of tension reflect the same sort of basic dynamics. It is the triangle of the father-mother-child relationship that supplies feeling for the relevance of the formal doctrines and accounts for the varying types of response to them. Who will say that the feeling for grace, love, and forgiveness as attributes of God is not derived from the mother? Or that Word as symbol of authority, will, judgment, freedom, and responsibility do not come from the father? Such observations as these emphasize the crucial importance of family religion in giving form and strength to belief.

value that may make it, in effect, an idol to which full devotion is given at the expense of other interests that make a full life. Out of this situation, costly and destructive conflict may arise. For example, the regulation of economic activities by free competition under the older order of free enterprise has long since become qualified by action of government to meet the increasing complexity of a kind of industrial production which threatened the access of the individual to free opportunity. Such opportunity in a democracy is a value higher than efficiency in production and warrants the imposition of restraints under the principle of the general welfare.

The older adage, "Keep the government out of business," first began to give way when business needed the assistance of government in developing and protecting enterprise. Then it had to yield further in the presence of organized economic power driving on toward an objective that involved the exploitation of individuals and ultimately threatened to undermine the stability of the whole economy. Conflict of interests needed to be resolved by controls that guaranteed universal opportunity and distribution of purchasing power. The illustration is sufficient to indicate that in a highly integrated society, there must always be some higher value, some normative standard by which particular interests are kept in balance and fruitfully active. In this situation, however, it is certainly conceivable that a government acting in behalf of individuals who, in their need, may become increasingly dependent on it, might itself usurp full power and form a totalitarian state. There must then be a value higher than the state that is normative for its conduct of affairs.

It is in the presence of this need that we discover the nature and mission of *the church*. When we speak of religion as "the art and the theory of the internal life" and arrive at the conclusion that the supreme end sought by the practice of this art is the fulfillment of man as person, we are led to an understanding of the abiding significance of the institutional arrangement designed to serve that end. We recognize, first, that the church is more than an institution parallel to and correlated with other institutions in the strict sociological sense. It can be studied from an external standpoint as a social object and its identifying marks may be listed. It has a structure of activities related to the spiritual needs of the community. But internally it expresses a continuing movement which carries the peculiar meanings associated with its origin and tested by the exigencies of man's journey through history. Flowing from this is a second fact. The church is a *believing* community whose concern transcends the particular interests and beliefs which rule industry, government, education, and the arts. It acknowledges relationship with all these but works in detachment from and above what is called the secular order. Its values are those of the family universalized. Its concern is with man as man, his predicament when he functions only as a self and loses his cosmic dimension as person under God.

For Christians, the Bible plays the leading part in this concern and shapes the form of this detachment. It is the deposit of an epoch long since closed and which therefore stands apart from the experience of modern men. It is a treasured record of human struggle in search for the highest and best. It is an epic of the soul. The action of God is at the center of the Bible, and it is there that the believer knows the meaning of encounter with the divine. Only in the context of the Scriptures may God be perceived as personal Object outside man. Other knowledge may supplement and support (or question) this experience, but the basic insights come from the Old and the New Testaments and take the form of a constellation of articulated beliefs to be preached, taught, and lived. The power of religion resides in propositions which are accepted as true and which enable the believer to stand over against the world, judge it, love it, and work for its redemption. In this way, he identifies himself with the work of God and knows himself, in that relationship, as one who is *in* the world but not *of* it. To live with this orientation is to look at human purpose and decisions "under the aspect of eternity," as Spinoza put it, and to advance beyond self into true personhood.

This description of complicated human activities, even in the brevity which we have imposed upon it, reveals clearly the transcendent fact of their interrelatedness, each affecting all others for better or for worse and altogether expressing man's cultural adventure. This interdependence is not the willed act of man, not in any sense his deliberate creation. In it, he is participant, but left to himself, he will resist it or exploit for private purposes the enormous opportunity which it offers to him as an individual. This interdependence is the work of God, expressing His grace toward man in the universal bounty of possibilities already actualized and with more beyond too great to be calculated. So far as we can see, looking at all the facts before us, it is the purpose of God to bring man to fulfillment as person, to complete His creation in him. Wherever there is crisis for personhood, there God is offering in Himself that value which transcends all other values and inviting men to revalue all cultural acts and to reconstitute them by the power of a supreme objective beyond them. This is the religious process. It should be emphasized, however, that God does not accomplish His purpose in man by coercion. It is by a free act of *devotion,* of inward resolution, continuous growth in redemptive insight, and dedication, that man advances in higher attainment as man. But this, as achievement in history, involves the ordeal of sustained inward decision leading to outward act in social reconstruction.

4. *God in the Ultimate Crisis of Man*

Whatever may be their divergence at particular points, science and biblical religion, in their final outcomes, complement each other in rounding out our view of what is ultimately at stake in the making of man. The one, by laborious research and descriptive reporting, discloses the events which mark his appearance on the earthly scene, and opens the way for inference regarding *his nature.* The other, through the vivid history of a particular people, leads to a conviction concerning *his worth* and his appropriate destiny. Both, in a manner peculiar to their basic orientations, announce the fact of struggle and sacrifice in actualizing any higher order of existence. Science views man's eminence in nature as the result of adaptive conquests extending over long ages of earth-time and involving passage through countless changing forms. The Bible starts with man's value to God and makes this normative in its account of nature.

From the call of Abraham to the last of the prophets, from Jesus to the vision of the New Jerusalem, the theme runs true through all variations. In the Old Testament, all events are in some way related to Yahweh's love for Israel. In the New, the climactic occasion is grounded in "God so loved the world." But in the biblical view of man, it is as clear as it is in science that the path of life leads upward only at the price of conflict in which the outreach for human self-completion engages the lower orders of man's being in unending contest between better and worse, right and wrong. It is more than metaphor to say that the road from Pilate's "judgment hall" to Golgotha is a recapitulation of all history in its convergence upon the central issue in all human living. In the few hours required to make that journey, time seems to stand still while earth's total past is relived. The voice of the mob echoes the mute clamor of primordial seas and the growl of the primeval jungle. Conscience, attained in the latter ages as the way out of the darkness of the instincts into the light of self-

consciousness, washes its hands. The honor of justice is be-
fouled by regresssion while remorse flickers in the soul of a
man going to "his own place." Faint hearts, powerless to
cope with the invasion of fear and unable effectively to
wield the sword, weep for their loss and spoken denial.

The four Evangelists spare no pains in setting forth the
words and acts of these "last days." Intuitively they perceive that a transaction of decisive consequence is taking
place, and subsequent history sustains their insight and
judgment. What is the heart of the message which they
impart? What is the "good news" that began in Galilee
and came fully to light amid the shadows of a place called
"a skull"? In a word, which we must amplify, the Cross
declares man's union with nature and his deliverance from
it through a supreme act of responsibility that satisfies the
ultimate purpose of freedom.

The death of Jesus, in the form which it took, must be
recognized, first, as the result of free, uncoerced decision.
The character of the final act cannot be discerned, of
course, apart from its place in the context of his previous
career. His baptism, his temptation in the wilderness, his
dealing with the challenge of his contemporaries, his teaching of the disciples, and all that expresses the supremacy
of his trust in God come to consummation upon the Cross.
Yet, it should be noted that, on every occasion which called
for choice, alternatives are open for changing his course.
He need not come to trial for heresy or sedition. Indeed,
he is not unalterably committed when he "steadfastly set
his face to go to Jerusalem." Gethsemane lies beyond where,

in prayer before the last step is taken, he weighs the issue and resists with earnest plea the "cup" set before him. Even at this hour, it is not too late to turn back, to renounce everything that has brought him into jeopardy. Such a course need not involve public or open disavowal of what he has stood for. He could, with the support of many others of his time, retire into pious asceticism and continue to wait for "the day of the Lord." A strategic retreat to rally the Zealots for armed resistance is another option which had been fruitful in the time of the Maccabees. Our point is that, until the moment when he submitted to arrest, Jesus' freedom to deal with external circumstances, in a manner favorable to his safety, is uncompromised. He is equally free to reject all that comes to mind from this source and take his final position on "not what I will, but what thou wilt." (Mark 14:36) It is here that we encounter the majesty of his inward character, now fully manifest in his power to make a decision that unites ultimate consequence with immediate occasion.

All the questions which surround the knotty problem of human freedom cannot be treated within the compass of our present purpose, but it is an issue that has emerged again and again as our thought has moved through these pages. In the main, we have considered the subject in the context of alternatives available in particular settings. Yet, even within such limits, it has been repeatedly apparent that human action, at any time, is subject to influences beyond the response indicated by the bare facts of the moment. In most cases, consequences are judged on the

basis of past experience, including what one has learned
from history. But in view of the fact that past events are
not precisely reproduced in subsequent situations, so that
what was wise in actions taken yesterday cannot be taken
as a literal guide today, an element of faith often, if not
invariably, affects decision. Our idea of freedom belongs in
the context of such considerations as these. We have related it to man's self-consciousness, his status as a creature
separated from his Creator and his endowment with special
powers suggested by the "image of God" in him. The
phrase "being true to oneself" did duty in our early dis-
cussions of the soul of Israel. The word "autonomy," in
varying ways, also indicated man's capacity to go his own
way. It would seem, then, that, in the design of God, the
freedom of man is grounded in the fact that it vastly multi-
plies the options of possibility for the unfolding of the
diversity and richness of His creative powers. In this, of
course, God takes the risk that human choices may run
counter to His purpose and delay or frustrate its realization.

Nevertheless, in the perspective that is guiding us, it is
clear that freedom is the attribute of man which makes
him of peculiar worth to God. That worth, evident in recurring crises of the biblical history, is declared without
ambiguity in the act of Jesus on the Cross and certified in
the accounts of his resurrection. In this act, Jesus is not
a victim sacrificed to appease the Divine wrath aroused by
man's use of freedom in disobedience. On the premises
which we have stated, God does not charge man with guilt
for making choices which, by His own act, were within the

range of possibility from the beginning. His boundless resources can withstand man's most sinful waste. The transcendent fact is that in Jesus it was possible for God, without renouncing His original wisdom, to reveal the love which had always accompanied it, but until then was only dimly perceived by men. This could happen because Jesus, by his own free choice, manifested the kind of responsibility that satisfied the full requirement of freedom and set its meaning forever before the mind of man. This responsibility transformed decision dictated by the prudential demands of the immediate situation into a decision that met the terms of God's purpose for all mankind. We are told that even the pagan mind, clouded by superstition, recognized the extraordinary character of this event. But those who had been nurtured by the intimate memories of earlier association could hear a higher voice saying, "Thou art my beloved son," and place the Cross at the center of the gospel they preached.

The event we have thus pursued has been interpreted in many ways, a fact which attests its importance in shaping attempts to deal with the problem of man.[6] For us, it yields,

---

[6] The theme which we are discussing here has counterparts in the writings of great literary artists who approach the problem of man from an inward perspective without theological orientation. In Shakespeare's tragedies, notably "Macbeth," we see the struggle of conscience, yielding in the end to ambition that violates a higher loyalty. In Dostoevski's *Brothers of Karamazov,* there is a passage (p. 321f) which announces that "we are all responsible to all for all, apart from our own sins."

Even more articulate is the statement of Peer Holm, Johan Bojer's hero in *The Great Hunger.* Here the inward struggle which follows

for all its mystery, what we have called "the majesty of the inward character" of our Lord. By this we mean that balance between fact and value, event and faith, which contributes to decision that fulfills the demands of all when set in the dimension of ultimate possibility. Beyond what seems to be authentic in the gospel narratives, we may not presume to know what was in the mind of Jesus in the last days. Yet, within bounds, inference can be drawn. We risk, with some assurance, two propositions. The history of his people, "the soul of Israel," was in him, palpably real in all the alternatives that had been tried before his time. We may be sure that he lived, especially, on the mountain of vision with Moses and the prophets. His contemporary world, marked by cultural interpenetration, the "Roman peace," and the Roman power over the Nation, was equally real.

Much of Jesus' interaction with this world is given in direct statement, simile, and parable. It is not necessary to say that all past and contemporary events were in his mind at once. But we may say that essential elements of the whole world, as he had inherited them and perceived

---

the death of Peer's little daughter, by the brutal attack of the brazier's wolf-dog, begins with desire for vengeance and ends with compassion. The brazier's land lies dry from drought, and angry neighbors will not sell him grain for replanting. Emerging from his inward battle, Peer remembers that he has some barley left. He rises in the night and sows it in the "enemy's" field. He explains his act by saying that he did it because, "standing on the ruins" of his life, he felt "a vast responsibility," and adds, "Mankind must be better than the blind powers that order its ways; in the midst of its sorrows, it must take heed that the godlike does not die." (Used by permission of Curtis Brown, Ltd. Copyright, 1919.)

them, were in him discriminately placed as fact and value. The clash and clamor of human conflict reverberated in his thought as he examined the issues. Inwardly, the resolution came with the sorting out of the ultimately right from the prudent and the expedient. He endured the travail of it as each decision led him on toward the end. God was at the center of each choice not as power to coerce but as test of right and strength to sustain.

At last the great act came as consummatory moment of all that had preceded it. He "emptied" himself of all that was local, attached to a particular time, place, and social condition. He became "servant," the greatest of all, in presenting free man to God in an act of responsibility commensurate with the most inclusive and exacting demands of freedom. This is the final step from self to person. When one can use his own human condition as the clue to the total human situation and, with the whole world in his heart, act with a sense of responsibility for all mankind, it is then that he bears the mark of true personhood. The anguish of so transcending self is explicit in the suffering of Jesus on the Cross.

In this perspective, the meaning of death becomes apparent. As a fact, though not the manner of its coming in particular cases, death is a part of the work of God and as integral to His purpose as birth. It presents to man constant challenge to delay it as long as possible, that life may attain its maximum tenure and fulfillment, and then, beyond that, incites him to use awareness of his mortality to understand the nature of his existence. Life begins and ends with a separation. But in the adventure that lies between, society nurtures a self which God Himself captures at the center for the making of a person. The self clings to the body as the scene of its social habitation. Reborn in personhood that unites responsibility with freedom, under God, it is deathless. Reclothed with "a spiritual body," the words and deeds which transcend self in a universe of meaning and value become a part of the world's enduring treasure.

> The creation waits with eager longing for the revealing of the sons of God.

> And this is eternal life, that they know thee the only true God, and Jesus Christ whom thou hast sent.

> Truly, truly, I say to you, he who *believes* has eternal life.[7]

Grief over separations in the sphere of the self is transformed by the union of the temporal with the eternal, by the transcendence of particular event through faith. Men and women whose visible pilgrimage comes to an end, "not having received the promises," live on as a "cloud of witnesses" in the blessed community of persons whose center is God, and whose witness is constant encouragement to continue the "race that is set before us." The church, as the "body of Christ," reclothes the mortal with immortality by nurturing decisions of the self to become person and to begin living here and now in the spacious "rooms" of the Father's house not made with hands.

---

[7] Romans 8:19, John 17:3; John 6:47 (RSV), respectively.

5. *The Discipline of Decision*

The power of decision is the supreme mark of man as self-conscious being. It stands at the peak of nature's upward climb and measures the distance of advance beyond chemical reaction and animal instinct. It is in decision that man, singly and collectively, knows who he is. Why is this so? In answer, it will be necessary only to review the principal elements which enter into an act of choice. First, every decision, even in its most elementary form, engages the past. Second, this past is reshaped by the demands of a new situation for which older responses are not adequate. Repetition, or drawing upon one's repertory of previous actions, often does duty for careful rethinking in order to economize effort and to get on with the day's work. But it is almost certain, except in the most mechanical routines, that other factors, not faced before, are present. Later developments frequently show up this fact and the deficiency in the previous action is recognized.

A third requirement of decision includes the operational functions of intelligence, memory, reason, and imagination, by which experience is mobilized, integrated, and consequences are projected. In this process, quantitative and qualitative factors appear. Questions of "how much?" and "of what kind?" are unavoidable, and their respective objectives, in thoughtful appraisal, tend to be antagonistic. One may say, "If I do this, I will have *more*, but the *value*, of my act, in terms of right and wrong, may be less." This is one source of the critical tension in decision. A fourth element brings us to the more basic concern of freedom and responsibility. Here the questions extend the range of possibility and intensify the conflict between alternatives. One may say, "I am free to do this, but *ought* I?" "Ought" lifts the issue above the level of immediate social judgment and consequence and subjects it to the test of a universal perspective. It suggests the question, "If I do this, will I be acting in a way that does justice to all that is involved in my true character as a man?" In this, the reference is to a norm deemed applicable to acts of all men, everywhere, and at all times. We reach, then, the conclusion that the crucial fact about decision is the degree of responsibility which it expresses.

By this test, as we have seen, Jesus led the way to the heights of manhood. In himself, he presented man to God in the fullness of that inward stature which matched responsibility with freedom in the measure which justified the divine wisdom in creating man. He was the final test of the work of God, declared in the beginning "very good," but now beyond the reach of adjective in decision and act so transparent and whole that to utter praise of him would be desecration. Behold the Person!

From the summit of this vision, which we have reached in our pursuit of the "art and the theory of the internal life," we must now descend to the lowlands, where men struggle with the realities of their daily existence, and ask our final questions. How may man, in the adventure of self becoming person, sustain that kind of responsibility which came to light in Jesus, and to which God responded with deepest mutuality of redemptive love that is His gift of grace to all mankind? How may men, in their highest vision of the possibility manifest in Jesus, find release from inward fragmentation and direction for Christian decision in the concrete situations where they are called upon to act? The assumptions underlying our study require an answer to these questions in terms that express the most distinctive discipline of religion. That discipline is worship.

Stated with utmost brevity, worship is the meeting of God with man on occasions marked by human readiness to respond to the divine initiative and purpose. Four essential elements of this experience are set forth in Isaiah 6:1-8 (RSV). The *first* of these is the coming of the Lord in vivid, sovereign Presence.

> I saw the Lord . . . high and lifted up; . . .
> And one called to another and said:
> "Holy, holy, holy is the Lord of hosts;
> the whole earth is full of his glory."

The *second* is the reaction to the Divine Presence acknowledging the human condition of separation from God in its bearing on the state of the individual and of the society to which he belongs.

> And I said: "Woe is me! For I am lost; for I am a man
> of unclean lips, and I dwell in the midst of a people
> of unclean lips; for my eyes have seen the King, the
> Lord of hosts!"

The *third* step is the divine act of purification and forgiveness following confession.

And he touched my mouth, and said:
  "Behold, this has touched your lips; your
  guilt is taken away, and your sin forgiven."

The *fourth* component of worship is the call to service
and the acceptance of responsibility.

And I heard the voice of the Lord saying,
  "Whom shall I send, and who will go for us?"

With this general pattern of thought about worship before us, we turn to a more explicit examination of its meaning, first, in relation to the individual, and then to the
believing community which is the church.

On its human side, worship is the search for orientation
toward life as a whole through readiness to respond to the
vision of God as transcendent Object. It begins with some
form of affirmation such as Paul expresses in Acts 17:27,
28—"that they should seek God, in the hope that they might
feel after him and find him. Yet he is not far from each
one of us, for 'In him we live and move and have our
being.'" In our language, this is the quest for completer
being as person. Without implying that they have significance apart from the total act of worship, we may set down
some of the further steps which enter into it. The first is
relaxation. In this, the self surrenders to the person in its
outreach for communication with God. This psychophysical
attitude is the invocation of private worship and may or
may not be put into words. It involves an open and expanded mental outlook without specific prescription of
what is being sought.

The second step is *recollection* which has a twofold character. Its function is to examine the behavior of the self. It is the process which identifies inner tendencies toward fragmentation, and exposes the conflict between ends that draw life into unity and those ends which create division and draw off the powers of the self into unstable, accidental, or fortuitous compromises. Another phase of recollection is the spontaneous entering into one's past, marking particularly hallowed moments when one felt close to God and significant decisions were made. One remembers also some great hour in other lives, some deliverance from a crisis in history, some stirring thought from the Bible or other literature.

The third step is the recognition of *dependence,* how one's life rests upon supports provided by a vast network of physical and social relations, and ultimately upon God, whose providence appears in countless ways, but is especially manifest in the testimony of a "cloud of witnesses" that gives us the feeling of being connected with what has been and with the "promises" of what will be. The fruit of dependence is gratitude.

From these, the mood of worship moves into *meditation.* This involves selection and association of ideas which grip the mind as one identifies his need. It passes into appreciation of meanings which come and then, finally, into the appropriation of insight for better living. This is the active, inward waiting to receive which gives us the sense of God seeking us rather than our striving after Him. This is the communion of host and Guest, the true enjoyment of the divine companionship, not for what we may do with it, but for what it does for us in delivering us from the fragmentation and loneliness of the self through renewing our personhood.

Imperceptibly, meditation leads to *prayer* or verbal communication with God. Now that one is ready, adoration of the Highest is possible. The spirit of thanksgiving is exultant. God is real, a living Presence. We found Him along the trail of recollection and meditation. We felt our dependence upon Him. Lo! now He is here in the fullness of our capacity to perceive Him, and we are prepared to speak to Him and to listen to Him. The wayward, anarchic impulse to assert part against whole, self against person, has now found its place in our total sense of being. We make our petition in the light of decision required by our responsibilities and opportunities for expanded usefulness in the day's work. In the amplitude of greater grasp of our obligation and our privilege, with vision clarified and strength renewed, we return to our tasks more sensitive to our neighbor's need and more resolved to seek the good of all mankind. We are more man than we were, with depth and rapture.

Not all occasions set for worship, attain this sense of oneness with God. The human adventure has its period of lull, of inward numbness, of "dryness." But one can always, in such moments, relive an awareness of God that came at some previous time, in some other setting when one was more sensitive to His presence, or when conditions within us were more favorable. He is in our history. He is with us in immediate event, though inner clouds may shut Him from view. We cannot always "mount up with wings as eagles" or "run and not be weary." But we can "walk and not faint" if ever in our past we have known the meaning of worship and drawn from it decision that steadily sustained us in subsequent living.

Assembly for worship, or common worship, includes all the elements which enter into private worship, but the occasion is of necessity more formal and deliberative with design to prepare a congregation for a visitation from God. But there are differences which must be emphasized. Most important is the fact that although the worshiper retains his character as a self, he is more susceptible to reactions in his character as a person than in any other situation. The bipolarity of God and man, in the experience, is the same as in private worship, but the kind of interaction that may get under way is enhanced in its range and intensity. The Otherness of the transcendent Object is accentuated by the setting of a sanctuary with peculiar appointments, by the liturgy and symbolism which accomplish with immediate result the internal changes we have mentioned. These have the effect of modifying the individuality and separation of the self and preparing it to yield to the transforming influence of the Divine.

The sharing of others in the experience of worship strengthens the response of the person in entering into communion with the Supreme Person. Isaiah's vision of the "Lord high and lifted up," the chant of "Holy, holy, holy . . . the whole earth is full of his glory," the cry of the self, "Woe is me!" as it waits for redemption, are explicit evidence of the point we are making. Add the support of other elements such as common praise, symbolic acts, and spoken prayers, and we have a composite of quiet power that touches the depths of the unconscious and subtly suffuses it with a peace that passes understanding. How startling is the contrast between the mood of a crowd obsessed with some selfish or cruel purpose and the mood of common worship! In the one, man is *driven* by primitive, irrational instinct; in the other, he is *drawn* by devotion, toward the heights of disciplined manhood.

In completing our description of common worship, some reference must be made to the place and function of the sermon and the sacraments. Although preaching is older than the church, it does not follow that it is indispensable. At its best, the sermon is integral with the mood of worship and contributes to the total act of the meeting of man with God. But it may be more divertive than supportive. Its perils arise, mainly, from the tendency of the self to distort the functioning of the person in the pulpit. This is the acme of paradox, for preaching is communication in discourse of a high order, and that also is within the basic meaning of being a person. If, therefore, the sermon is to be useful it must submit to the discipline imposed by the objective of the occasion. Its content must be the message committed to the Church, spoken with the vital touch of insight and courage and warmed by sincere conviction, but void of what is eccentric, showy, and transient. Its service is to deal with "that which is permanent in the nature of things," meaning, in this context, God in Christ "reconciling the world to himself." As the liturgy and objective symbols evoke organic emotional response of the congregation, the sermon, combining feeling with reason and persuasion, articulates the convictions which give form and urgency to decision.

In Protestantism, the sacraments of baptism and the Lord's Supper are viewed in varying theological perspectives, but the common meaning resides in their character as acts of participation in the life and death of Christ. Both are celebrations of historic events which stand at the center of faith.

Baptism expresses that initial decision by which one surrenders the self and yields to the transformation of Christlike personhood, uniting the freedom of wholehearted choice with responsibility for contributing to the universal witness of the Church. It is active commitment to the discipline of Christian nurture in association with others who are similarly motivated.

The Communion of the Lord's Supper confronts the believer with the total life of Jesus Christ as it converged upon the Cross and there, joining free act with responsibility in a universal dimension, became God's act of revelation concerning the consummation of His purpose in creating man. Remembrance of Christ institutes searching inquiry on the part of the believer whereby he identifies his need for renewal and, accepting the grace of God bestowed in Christ, is led, in overflowing gratitude, to repeated decision and rededication to the divine will.

In briefest survey, these are the meanings of worship in terms of their bearing upon the making of man. In both its forms, private and common, it is grounded in beliefs, or formulations of truth, accepted as valid directives for transforming human living. In both settings, the complete act, engaging the total personality, is a recapitulation or a reliving of previous experience, oriented toward a transcendent Object in whose Presence alternatives are appraised and decision is freely made and sustained in integrity of purpose. Stated in another way, the community of believers nurtures the "I-me" of the individual, in which the "me" is internalized society and the "I" is reaction to that experience, and prepares the composite of both for the fuller dimension of personhood through active relation with "Thou," the God and Father of our Lord Jesus Christ. It is by worship that man becomes whole, gathers the disparate elements of his self into the unity of personhood and renews his powers for the work of transmuting his existing community into the kingdom of God.

BIBLIOGRAPHY

Albright, William F. *Archeology and the Religion of Israel.* Baltimore: The Johns Hopkins Press, 1942.

Alexander, Franz, and French, Thomas M. *Studies in Psychosomatic Medicine: An Approach to the Cause and Treatment of Vegetative Disturbances.* New York: The Ronald Press Company, 1948.

Allee, W. C. *The Social Life of Animals.* New York: W. W. Norton & Company, Inc., 1938.

Allport, Gordon W. *The Individual and His Religion.* New York: The Macmillan Company, 1951.

Berry, R. J. A. *Your Brain and Its Story.* London, New York: Oxford University Press, 1939.

Bible, The. The Authorized and Revised Standard Versions and the Moffatt Translation. New York: American Bible Society, Thomas Nelson & Sons, 1953. George H. Doran Company, 1922.

Bojer, Johan. *The Great Hunger.* London and New York: Curtis Brown, Ltd., 1919.

Boring, Edwin G. et al. *Psychology.* New York: John Wiley & Sons, Inc., 1935.

Bretall, Robert, ed. *A Kierkegaard Anthology.* Princeton: Princeton University Press, 1951.

Brunner, Emil. *God and Man.* London: Student Christian Movement Press, 1936.

———. *The Divine-Human Encounter.* Philadelphia: The Westminster Press, 1943.

Bultmann, Rudolph. *Theology of the New Testament,* Vol. I. New York: Charles Scribner's Sons, 1951.

Cadoux, Cecil J. *The Historic Mission of Jesus.* New York: Harper & Brothers, 1941.

Dibelius, Martin. *Jesus.* Translated by C. B. Hedrick and F. C. Grant. Philadelphia: The Westminster Press, 1949.

Dodd, C. H. *The Epistle of Paul to the Romans.* New York: Harper & Brothers, 1932.

———. *Gospel and Law.* New York: The Columbia University Press, 1951.

Dollard, John, and Miller, N. E. *Personality and Psychotherapy.* New York: McGraw-Hill Book Company, 1950.

Doniger, Simon, ed. *Religion and Human Behavior.* New York: Association Press, 1954.

———. *The Best in Pastoral Psychology.* Great Neck: Pastoral Psychology Press, 1952.

Dunbar, Flanders. *Mind and Body: Psychosomatic Medicine.* New York: Random House, 1947.

Eddington, Sir Arthur. *The Nature of the Physical World.* New York: The Macmillan Company, 1928.

Einstein, Albert, and Infeld, Leopold. *The Evolution of Physics.* New York: Simon and Schuster, Inc., 1938.

English, O. S., and Pearson, H. J. *Emotional Problems of Living.* New York: W. W. Norton & Company, Inc., 1945.

Ellenburg-Wiener, Renée von. *Fearfully and Wonderfully Made.* New York: The Macmillan Company, 1938.

Farrer, Austin. *A Study in Mark.* New York: Oxford University Press, 1952.

Fosdick, H. E. *On Being a Real Person.* New York: Harper & Brothers, 1943.

Frank, L. K. *Nature and Human Nature.* New Brunswick: Rutgers University Press, 1951.

Fromm, Erich. *Psychoanalysis and Religion.* New Haven: Yale University Press, 1950.

———. *The Forgotten Language.* New York: Rinehart & Company, Inc., 1951.

———. *Man For Himself.* New York: Rinehart & Company, Inc., 1947.

Gray, George W. *The Advancing Front of Science.* New York: Whittlesey House, 1937.

————. *The Advancing Front of Medicine.* New York: Whittlesey House, 1941.

Herrick, C. J. *Brains of Rats and Men.* Chicago: University of Chicago Press, 1926.

————. *The Thinking Machine.* Chicago: University of Chicago Press, 1929.

Hiltner, Seward. *Self-Understanding.* New York: Charles Scribner's Sons, 1951.

Hughes, Margaret M., ed. *The People in Your Life.* New York: Alfred A. Knopf, Inc., 1952.

Ibsen, Henrik. *Peer Gynt.* New York: Charles Scribner's Sons, 1916.

Ingham, H. V., and Love, L. R. *The Process of Psychotherapy.* New York: McGraw-Hill Book Company, Inc., 1954.

Irwin, William A. *The Old Testament—Keystone of Human Culture.* New York: Henry Schuman, 1952.

Jennings, H. S. *The Biological Basis of Human Nature.* New York: W. W. Norton & Company, Inc., 1930.

Jung, C. G. *The Integration of Personality.* New York: Farrar & Rinehart, Inc., 1939.

Kempf, E. J. *Psychopathology.* St. Louis: The C. V. Moser Company, 1921.

Maves, Paul B., ed. *The Church and Mental Health.* New York: Charles Scribner's Sons, 1953.

May, Rollo. *Man's Search for Himself.* New York: W. W. Norton & Company, Inc., 1953.

McCasland, S. V. *By the Finger of God.* New York: The Macmillan Company, 1951.

Mead, G. H. *Mind, Self and Society.* Chicago: University of Chicago Press, 1934.

Oates, Wayne E. *The Bible and Pastoral Care.* Philadelphia: The Westminster Press, 1953.

Orlinsky, H. M. *Ancient Israel.* Ithaca: Cornell University Press, 1954.

Overstreet, H. A. *The Great Enterprise.* New York: W. W. Norton & Company, Inc., 1952.

Parsons, Ernest W. *The Religion of the New Testament*. New York: Harper & Brothers, 1939.

Pedersen, Johannes. *Israel: Its Life and Culture*, Vol. I and II. London: Oxford University Press, 1926.

Pfeiffer, Robert H. *Introduction to the Old Testament*. New York: Harper & Brothers, 1941.

Poteat, E. M. *God Makes the Difference*. New York: Harper & Brothers, 1951.

Roberts, David E. *Psychotherapy and a Christian View of Man*. New York: Charles Scribner's Sons, 1950.

Romer, Alfred S. *Man and the Vertebrates*. Chicago: University of Chicago Press, 1953.

Sartre, Jean-Paul. *Existential Psychoanalysis*. New York: Philosophical Library, 1953.

Schaer, Hans. *Religion and the Cure of Souls in Jung's Psychology*. New York: Pantheon Books, Inc., 1950.

Shapley, Harlow. *Galaxies*. Cambridge: The Blakiston Company, Inc., 1943.

Sherrington, Sir Charles. *Man on His Nature*. New York: The Macmillan Company, 1941.

Sigerist, Henry E. *Civilization and Disease*. Ithaca: Cornell University Press, 1943.

Smith, C. R. *The Bible Doctrine of Man*. London: Epworth Press, 1951.

Stevers, Martin. *Mind Through the Ages*. New York: Doubleday, Doran Company, 1940.

Tillich, Paul. *The Courage to Be*. New Haven: Yale University Press, 1952.

Trueblood, D. Elton. *The Predicament of Modern Man*. New York: Harper & Brothers, 1944.

White, William A. *Outlines of Psychiatry*. Washington: Nervous and Mental Disease Publishing Company, 1926.

Whitehead, Alfred N. *Religion in the Making*. New York: The Macmillan Company, 1926.

Williams, Daniel D. *What Present Day Theologians Are Thinking*. New York: Harper & Brothers, 1952.

INDEX